Writers of Wales

Jane Williams (Ysgafell)

Editors:

Jane Aaron

M. Wynn Thomas

Andrew Webb

Honorary Series Editor:

R. Brinley Jones

Meic Stephens†

Other titles in the Writers of Wales series:
Hester Lynch Thrale Piozzi (2020), Michael John Franklin
Christopher Meredith (2018), Diana Wallace
B. L. Coombes (2017), Bill Jones and Chris Williams
Owen Rhoscomyl (2016), John S. Ellis
Dylan Thomas (2014), Walford Davies
Gwenlyn Parry (2013), Roger Owen
Welsh Periodicals in English 1882–2012 (2013), Malcolm Ballin
Ruth Bidgood (2012), Matthew Jarvis
Dorothy Edwards (2011), Claire Flay
Kate Roberts (2011), Katie Gramich
Geoffrey of Monmouth (2010), Karen Jankulak
Herbert Williams (2010), Phil Carradice
Rhys Davies (2009), Huw Osborne
R. S. Thomas (2006), Tony Brown
Ben Bowen (2003), T. Robin Chapman
James Kitchener Davies (2002), M. Wynn Thomas

Writers of Wales

Jane Williams (Ysgafell)

Gwyneth Tyson Roberts

University of Wales Press
2020

www.uwp.co.uk

British Library Cataloguing-in-Publication Data
A catalogue record for this book is available from the British Library.

ISBN 978-1-78683-563-5
e-ISBN 978-1-78683-564-2

The University of Wales Press acknowledges the financial assistance of the Books Council of Wales in the publication of this book.

Typeset in Wales by Eira Fenn Gaunt, Cardiff
Printed by CPI Antony Rowe, Chippenham, Wiltshire

To all the friends in Aberystwyth, London, Pembrokeshire and Swansea
who over the years have continued to ask how my work on
Jane Williams was going, and then listened patiently to the answer

Jane Williams (Ysgafell), *c*.1870
Supplied by Llyfrgell Genedlaethol Cymru/
National Library of Wales.

Contents

Acknowledgements

Many people have helped in different ways in the research for, and writing of, this book and I am grateful to all of them, especially Jane Aaron, Martin Davies, David Evans, Simon French, Katie Gramich, John Grenfell, Ann Trevenen Jenkin, Richard Marggraf Turley, Louise Marshall, Paulette Pelosi, Sarah Prescott and Susan Sidgwick.

I am also grateful to the staffs of the following: British Library, Carmarthenshire Archives, Centre for Kentish Studies, Chelsea and Kensington Archives, City of Westminster Archives, Florence Nightingale Museum, Guildhall Library, Hackney Archives, Herefordshire Record Office, Inverness Record Office, Lincolnshire Archives, London Metropolitan Archives, Medway Archives, National Archives (Kew), North Devon Record Office, Portsmouth Record Office, Powys County Archives, Royal Naval Museum Library, Shropshire Regimental Museum, Society of Genealogists, and West Sussex Record Office. I am particularly grateful to the staff of Aberystwyth University Library and, above all, to the staff of the National Library of Wales, which holds much of the material on Jane Williams which has survived the last 150 years.

Abbreviations

ADM	Admiralty Files (held at National Archives, Kew, London)
Chelsea tax books	Chelsea Poor Rate tax books (held at Kensington and Chelsea Archives, London)
GPC	*Geiriadur Prifysgol Cymru* (Caerdydd; Gwasg Prifysgol Cymru, 1999–2002)
Iolo MSS	see Taliesin Williams in Bibliography
LD/FNM	Florence Nightingale's Nurses' Register (held at Florence Nightingale Museum, St Thomas's Hospital, London)
NLW	National Library of Wales
OED	*Oxford English Dictionary* (Oxford; Clarendon Press, 1933)
PCC	Prerogative of the Court of Canterbury (of Wills: available online)
PR	Parish Register
PROB	Probate (re PCC Wills)
RLF	Royal Literary Fund MS Loan 96, 1/1841.
Tonn MSS 3.109A	Letters from Hall to William Rees of Llandovery (publisher) re. the publication of *Artegall* (held in Cardiff Central Library).

Illustrations

1

Becoming a Writer

In 1824 Jane Williams (not yet 'Ysgafell') published her first book, *Miscellaneous Poems*. She was eighteen.

She had been born in Chelsea (on 1 February 1806) into an affluent middle-class family,[1] and until her mid-teens had lived in London and in towns in southern England; but then her family lost its money and moved to rural Breconshire. The change in the family fortunes required her to become self-supporting, and she went to live with another family a few miles from her own, apparently to look after their children.

She had crossed the deep social divide between those who employed other people to work in their homes, and those who were employed to work in the homes of others – and had crossed that divide downwards. She was dependent on her employers for the food she ate and the roof over her head; she needed to obey their orders and win their good will. The house she lived in was their home, not hers; the home she had shared with her own family no longer existed. Until her mid-teens she had lived in bustling urban areas but now she was in a house deep in the countryside, surrounded by fields; the only lane out was crossed by a ford which often flooded in winter, preventing access to the main road which led to the rest of the world and leaving her marooned with the family she worked for.[2]

Her life – and her life-chances – had changed dramatically, catastrophically and, it seemed, permanently. She could expect to spend her future life working for others, her own wishes and ambitions buried under the need to be an efficient and trustworthy servant to whatever employers fate brought her, who might be sympathetic and considerate but who equally well might be demanding and oppressive.

At that point in her life, to self-publish a collection of poems was a declaration – to the world and to herself – that she was neither a servant nor a child-minder, and that she refused to be defined by the situation into which circumstances had forced her. Instead, she had chosen her own identity; the publication of *Miscellaneous Poems* declared that she was a *writer*.

Jane Williams's writing career spanned more than half a century (roughly, the second and third quarters of the nineteenth century) and a wide range of genres: poetry, essays on religious subjects, fiction, an analysis of the 1847 Report on education in Wales, biography, a memoir of a childhood game, the 'autobiography' of someone else, literary criticism and academic history. Each of these two facts on its own – her longevity as an author and the range of genres in which she worked – was unusual for a woman writer in the nineteenth century; together they make her truly remarkable. She and her writing deserve more attention than they have received.

The relative lack of popular interest during her lifetime is most clearly explained by contrasting her life and work with those of two other women authors of the same generation whose writing attracted much more attention than hers, and much greater commercial success. Like Williams, both Anna Jameson (1794-1864) and Louisa Stuart Costello (1799-1870) came from middle-class family backgrounds whose lack of money meant they had to be self-supporting from their mid-teens and, also like her, while they wrote some poetry and fiction they were best known for their serious non-fiction: Jameson for writing on the art of the Italian Middle Ages and Renaissance, Costello for the history and literature of medieval France and Italy.[3] Their lives and writing, however, shared two important factors which Williams's lacked. Firstly, they cultivated networks of friends and contacts who were influential in English, London-based, literary circles; secondly, in an age which made a virtue of self-improvement, their books enabled members of the English middle classes (and members of the English working class who aspired to rise socially) to become knowledgeable about aspects of high culture.

Jameson had studied Italian medieval and Renaissance art during visits to Italy as chaperone and governess; later she moved in the same circles as Thomas and Jane Carlyle, Robert and Elizabeth Barrett Browning, and Elizabeth Gaskell (who asked her for advice on the ending of *North and South*).[4] Costello, who wrote that it was 'impossible to succeed in any [literary] endeavour – especially for a woman – unless some powerful friend would lend a pitying hand to help her', sent carefully flattering letters to influential literary figures (Sir Walter Scott, Thomas Moore, Maria Edgeworth, George Crabbe) which gained her publishing contracts, favourable reviews, and a pension for life.[5]

Williams fell short in both respects. She had no such 'powerful friend' in the London literary world; when, towards the end of her life, she needed the most impressive literary referees possible to support her application for financial help to the Royal Literary Fund, she could call only on minor writers (Geraldine Jewsbury and Anna Maria Hall) – authors who needed influential literary support themselves.[6] And in contrast to the subjects chosen by Jameson and Costello, which were both culturally impressive and socially useful to a wide range of English readers, most of Williams's published work was about Wales – and members of the English middle classes have never regarded a detailed and extensive knowledge of Welsh history and culture as necessary to prove their mental cultivation or aesthetic sensibilities.[7]

This lack of literary interest during Williams's lifetime has led to a similar neglect since her death. She left her personal and literary papers to her executors in the apparent hope of a biography[8] – and certainly, a book which used her papers and the memories of her family and friends would have put much useful material into the public domain. This did not happen, however, and her papers were dispersed and (mainly) lost.[9] As a result, her posthumous fate was the shadowy half-life of a writer whose works were out of print and whose existence was for many years only marked by short entries in reference books. And in some reference books her range of genres worked to her disadvantage, since her writing overall resisted tidy classification; descriptions of her as a 'miscellaneous writer', or – even less helpfully – an 'authoress', trivialise her work and are so uninformative that few casual readers are likely to want to track down her books for themselves.[10] Further, some compilers of reference books have confused her with two other, more or less contemporary, women of the same name and describe her wrongly as a 'musician' or a 'friend of Shelley' – mistakes which blur her image even further.[11] Other entries on her, and articles based on them, show a similar degree of inaccuracy, confusion and reliance on the compilers' assumptions. As a result, her image as an author is both indistinct and dull (I have discussed some of these inaccuracies in Appendix 1.)

The genres in which she wrote provide another explanation for the neglect of her writing. While the work of some nineteenth-century women authors (notably Jane Austen, the Brontë sisters, George Eliot, Elizabeth Barrett Browning) later became an established part of the English literary canon, it took some time for writing by other nineteenth-century women to attract serious critical attention, and that attention was initially directed to writers working in the same genres as those who had already made the grade: fiction and poetry. Since these two genres accounted for most of the writing published by women in Britain in the nineteenth century, this was not surprising; but it was bad news for women writers like Williams whose writing fell mainly within the general category of 'serious non-fiction'.[12] The Welsh subjects of her writing have been another cause of the neglect of her work. It is only comparatively recently that the study of Welsh writing in English has begun to extend its scope to women who wrote before the twentieth century[13]; a nineteenth-century writer like Jane Williams came very late to the party.

In her application to the Royal Literary Fund Jane Williams described herself as 'Welsh by descent and long residence'.[14] Like many self-descriptions, this is accurate as far as it goes but does not go very far; both her ancestry and the history of her residence are more complex, and more interesting, than the brief phrase implies. Her parents both came from families whose trajectories from the mid-eighteenth century to the mid-nineteenth show remarkable degrees of geographical, social and financial mobility – but not always in the direction they would have hoped.

William Marsh, her maternal grandfather, was a self-made rich man. He grew up in rural Middlesex in the middle of the eighteenth century, one of the younger sons of his father's second marriage (and therefore unlikely to inherit anything much). Like a pantomime hero he went to London to make his fortune – and did, as an investment banker. His younger brother Robert was equally successful as a purser in the Royal Navy, eventually becoming purser of the flagship of the Channel Fleet during the war against revolutionary France. Pursers who had good credit lines could make a lot of money for their investors; William and Robert worked together, to their mutual financial benefit.[15]

William and his wife Eleanor (née Unwin) lived in the City of London, above his banking offices. Of the eight children born to them only four – two sons and two daughters – survived to adulthood. Eleanor died shortly after the birth of their youngest child, named Eleanor after her (who became Jane Williams's mother). Three years later William married a woman from his home parish of Willesden who was fifteen years younger than himself: Jane (Stalker), after whom Jane Williams was later named.[16] By his will (made shortly before he died, aged forty-one) William's surviving children were to share his fortune equally, under the direction of his brother Robert (since leaving William's money to his wife Jane would have put it at the mercy of her second husband if she remarried). Robert moved the family to 35 Sloane Square in the (then) village of Chelsea;[17] he invested William's money carefully and, with no dependents of his own, added the proceeds of his own financially successful career to William's legacy. The shares of William's fortune for his sons were used to educate them and establish them in business; by his will, the two daughters, Elizabeth and Eleanor, were to receive their shares when William's youngest surviving child, Eleanor, turned twenty-one.[18] When she was eighteen, Robert died at sea[19]; the result was that on Eleanor's twenty-first birthday the two sisters were in the unusual position for women of their time in having access to their own money without it being under the control of a father or husband.

The family fortunes of Jane Williams's father David followed a very different trajectory. For centuries his paternal family owned a large estate in Montgomeryshire, to the west of Newtown; in the seventeenth century it was the home of Henry Williams (still mentioned in some histories of Wales as an example of a persecuted Puritan minister[20]). It descended to Jane Williams's paternal grandfather (another Henry Williams) who sold it, to his children's anger and resentment; in return his will threatened to disinherit them if they were so 'disobedient' and 'undutiful' as to continue to protest at the sale. (This was an empty threat, since he was so heavily in debt that he had little to leave to anyone; Jane Williams's paternal grandfather seems to have been as good at spending money as her maternal grandfather was at making it[21].) The estate had been rented out on a long lease, but – crucially for Jane Williams – if it had not been sold her father would have inherited it and her life would have been very different.[22]

The name of the estate – so important in the family's history and so resentfully lost for ever – was Ysgafell. When Jane Williams – who, apparently, never saw it – later chose it as her bardic name, her decision showed how large the estate loomed in her paternal family's history, and how profound was her sense of her family's loss of social status, affluence and the ownership of a piece of the land of Wales. Its name meant little outside her immediate circle, but choosing it to identify herself was a way of reclaiming by her pen the moral and emotional ownership of the estate which her grandfather had irrevocably sold out of the family.

David Williams was born and grew up on a much smaller estate, at Evenjobb in the parish of Old Radnor, a short walk from the border with England, which had come into the Williams family via his mother.[23] After she died (when he was fifteen) his father moved to a rented house in Whitney, a few miles north of Hay-on-Wye and just on the English side of the border (presumably to make some money by renting out the Evenjobb estate).[24] When David was seventeen he joined the Ticket Office of the Navy Office at its London headquarters in the Strand as a clerk; he got the job through a brother-in-law who was also a cousin (almost inevitably, another Henry Williams).[25] He is likely to have been able to exist on his low salary only by living with his eldest sister Anne and her husband in Westminster – and Anne was a friend of the Marsh sisters.[26] Eleanor Marsh and David Williams were married in March 1803 shortly after his twenty-first birthday, which meant that he did not need anyone's permission to marry (Eleanor had turned twenty-one – and inherited her share of her father's and uncle's money – the previous year). He moved to live with his wife, her sister and their stepmother at 35 Sloane Square; as a man he immediately became the head of the household although he was the youngest member of the family there, and by far the poorest.[27]

Over the following seventeen years Eleanor and David Williams had eight children: five daughters (one of whom died in infancy) and three sons. Jane was the second child and eldest daughter, born when her family was living in Sloane Square; David Williams's work later saw him posted to the naval bases at Portsmouth and Sheerness in Kent before returning to the headquarters of the Navy Office in the Strand.[28] The Williams family chose to live in Chelsea again, this time at 12 Riley Street.[29]

While very little information about Jane Williams's early life has survived, the subjects of the poems in her first collection show that she had a good education – especially for a girl at that period – and was given the opportunity to develop her intellectual interests. Although her father's salary remained low – he spent his entire working life as a Clerk Third Class, ninth on the list of Third-Class Clerks in the Ticket Office[30] – the income from the investments her mother had inherited from the Marsh brothers gave the Williams family an affluent middle-class lifestyle. Jane Williams later said that she had grown up 'in comfort, even luxury', and there was no reason to think that the rest of her life would be different.[31] But in

1820, when she was fourteen, financial disaster struck; her family lost most of its money.

The Williams family seems later to have wanted to forget this period as much as possible, and there is very little information about them between the end of June 1820, when they left Riley Street in Chelsea very suddenly[32], and April 1824 when Jane Williams wrote the Preface to *Miscellaneous Poems* from Pipton Cottage in Glasbury.[33] One possibility is that they spent some time with David Williams's relatives (two sisters and a brother-in-law) in the village of Clifford, north of Hay-on-Wye on the English side of the border.[34] A disproportionate number of the subscribers to her book were members of social and business networks in the Whitney–Clifford–Hay–Glasbury–Talgarth area and also investors or board members of the Brecon to Hay railway.[35] Lady Hereford, whose name heads the list of subscribers, was the wife of the board's chairman, and Lord Ashburnham, the owner of Aberenig House near Talgarth, where the Williams family lived for some years, was also an investor.[36]

In Pipton Cottage, Jane Williams was living with the Morgans (who eventually had nine children[37]); the only references to her time there appear in the Preface to *Miscellaneous Poems* and the poems themselves.

Publishing *Miscellaneous Poems* by subscription is more likely to have been a matter of necessity than choice for Williams. While many nineteenth-century female authors began their careers with a collection of poetry, the subscription method of publication was used far less often than in the previous century, and by the time Williams's book appeared it had become a notably unfashionable method – but useful for authors with little money.[38]

As well as Williams's family and friends, the list of subscribers includes members of the local 'great and good': major landowners, the local MP, and four Anglican clergymen (one of whom was the only subscriber from a Talgarth address, which suggests that she and her family were not well known there). In spite of the view of many people at this period that publishing one's poetry was unbecoming for a well-brought-up young woman, Williams not only used her own name on the title page rather than publishing anonymously or pseudonymously, but used her full name rather than an asexual initial for her first name. Declaring herself to be the book's author was clearly important to her.

The wide-ranging metre and rhyme schemes of the twenty poems are all handled with a degree of competence which suggests considerable practice. As one would expect in a young poet's first collection, the choice of subjects and approach reflect her reading: specifically, the work of eighteenth-century poets and their practice of quoting and echoing phrases from earlier poetry.[39] The influence of the work of Thomas Gray, Samuel Johnson and William Shenstone is particularly strong; the title of one poem ('A Pastoral, in imitation of Shenstone') makes her debt overt, while her poems include verbal echoes and near-quotations from Gray and Johnson. Two of her poems ('The Moss' and 'Gwernyfed Hall') echo phrases from Gray's 'Elegy Written in a Country Churchyard', while her poem 'Revenge', like Johnson's 'The Vanity of Human Wishes', supports its argument with examples from Classical and medieval history while advocating Christian forgiveness, and does so in the rhyming iambic pentameters of Johnson's poem. More than these specific examples, her poems reflect the note of graveyard melancholy found in much English (and Welsh) verse of the mid- and later eighteenth century: for example, 'The Peasant Maiden's Grave', 'On a Withered Rose', 'The Moss' (which covers graves beneath a 'mournful yew') and 'On the Trunk of an Old Tree' (which was once 'the pride of [the] green wood' but is now withered and covered by moss and ivy). In several of these poems the speaker, like many eighteenth-century predecessors, seeks solitude to meditate on the change and decay inherent in all earthly things and on the inevitable end of power, ambition, 'pomp and grandeur'.[40] The echoes of familiar poetic themes and vocabulary, together with Classical and other learned references, assured readers that the young author was writing in a well-established – masculine – literary tradition rather than producing the lighter, more sentimental verse which some male readers expected from women poets.

The volume says nothing about the dates or order of the poems' composition. However, 'On the Death of the Celebrated Napoleon Buonaparte' [*sic*] (which – typically – offers an example of the inevitable end of worldly ambition and power) was clearly written shortly after news of his death reached Britain in 1821, and 'Lines on the Banks of the Llunvey' and 'Gwernyfed Hall', on places in the Glasbury area, were composed after Williams moved there. Further, there is a significant contrast between the characterisation of Edward I in 'Revenge' (in which 'his glorious reign' is marred only by his invasion of Scotland) and the last poem in the collection, 'A Welsh Bard's Lamentation for the Death of the Last Llewellyn [*sic*] Prince of Wales'. The reference to Edward in 'Revenge' focuses entirely on 'Caledonia's woe' and in reading it one would never know that Edward I came anywhere near Wales; in 'A Welsh Bard's Lamentation', by contrast, 'the haughty Edward['s] . . . foreign ruffians' bring 'wretched slavery' and 'strife' to the Welsh people. Between the composition of the two poems, Williams had clearly read some Welsh history.

'Gwernyved Hall', one of the Welsh poems of place, is one of the group which reflects with melancholy on the change and decay of all earthly things, lost happiness, and the passing of 'pomp and grandeur'; it describes a visit in the moonlight to a 'mansion, [now] dark and grey' which had once been the place of 'mirthful cheer', of minstrels' 'jovial songs' and of 'youthful pairs' dancing to 'music's gay inspiring strain'. It would be interesting to know whether Williams had read English translations of early Welsh poetry by the time she wrote 'Gwernyfed Hall'; certainly her poem echoes the theme – and images – of the desolate and deserted hall in eighteenth-century translations of the ninth- and tenth-century elegies for Cynddylan and Urien Rheged.[41]

Gwernyfed Hall's fate would have had an additional resonance for Williams if she had read the history of its previous owners – which, given her interest in the history of her surroundings, is highly likely. It had been built in the reign of Elizabeth I as the seat of a rich and powerful gentry family. In 1731 it was partially gutted by fire and its owners moved to their other estate (in Norfolk) rather than rebuild it – so, to quote her poem's last line, 'pomp and grandeur. . .[had] fled' literally as well as metaphorically.

The surname of the family which owned the Hall during its period of power and affluence in the early seventeenth century was Williams; its head was Sir David (a rich and successful judge on the King's Bench), while his wife was Eleanor and their son and heir was Henry – that is, they had the first names of Jane Williams's father, mother and eldest brother. Williams was also the surname of the family who had owned the house in the later seventeenth and early eighteenth centuries; its most prominent members had been Edward and Elizabeth, the names of Jane Williams's second brother and second sister.[42] Set against the pomp and affluence of Gwernyfed's previous residents, the neglected state of the Hall when Jane Williams saw it was a vivid illustration of 'life's uncertain lot' (as she phrased it) in general; but although her family had no connection with the Williamses of Gwernyfed Hall, the coincidence that her own close relatives shared the names of the Hall's earlier occupants must have made it a symbol for her of the contrast between past happiness and present desolation – and evoked the loss of Ysgafell. In the countryside around Talgarth and Glasbury there were many reminders of the historical past – ruined castles, the remains of motte-and-baileys, the sites of ancient forts, tumuli, standing stones – but the only one known to have moved her to poetry was the one connected with a family whose fate inevitably recalled her own.

The other Welsh poem of place, 'Lines on the Banks of the Llunvey', also gives very personal significance to a conventional subject: the contrast between a river flowing smoothly in summer and 'raging' violently during winter storms. While treating the natural world as a mirror of the poet's feelings was a familiar literary device, the poem rejects the conventional conclusion: that summer will return and the river will again flow 'softly, sweetly'. Instead, its final stanza expects only storms and unhappiness:

> And thus does grief shed o'er the soul,
> Its wild, its terrible control,

And buries, in its dread abyss,
The peaceful form of happiness.

That 'the peaceful form of happiness' is 'burie[d] in [grief's] dread abyss' suggests that there is no hope of change; grief will exert 'its wild, its terrible control' for ever. The image is one of total despair, and the violent connotations of 'wild', 'terrible' and 'dread' present the river as a reminder of loss and emotional pain.

A small group of untitled poems seems even more openly autobiographical; one in particular apparently refers to the family disasters of the previous years. Its first line , 'Sink not my soul, oh! sink not in despair', establishes it as a monologue in which the 'I' lists all the reasons why the soul might understandably fall into despair while urging against it. The reasons for despair include 'many sad misfortunes', that 'hope of this world's happiness has flown', that 'Poverty' has arrived and 'Want stands ready with her frightful train', that the soul must 'resign' 'fondly cherished hopes' and part from 'best beloved friends', and face not only grief and illness but the 'scornful glance' of the proud which 'may chill my heart'. The list is formidable and even if one allows for the exaggerations of a self-dramatising adolescent (the 'hope of this world's happiness has flown', for example) the distress is real.

But the answer, says the 'I,' is to 'think on the Saviour's sufferings here below', beside which all human sufferings are nothing, and to pray to him in 'thy pain'. Williams demonstrated a strong religious faith throughout her life, and the attitude to suffering and hardship expressed in 'Sink not my soul. . .' would have been the only response possible for her. The result, however, is that the references to Christ's sufferings shut off firmly and permanently any further thought of her own very real distress which the first part of the poem describes.

This closing-down of an expression of personal suffering in 'Sink not, my soul' makes the last poem in the collection, 'A Welsh Bard's Lamentation for the Death of the Last Llewellyn [*sic*] Prince of Wales', particularly interesting. The first forty-two lines of the poem describe the events leading to Llywelyn's death (clumsily, as if information from history books had been only recently read and inadequately assimilated). They deal with the mustering of Llywelyn's troops near Builth, his betrayal by Mortimer to the English forces and his death in an ambush at the hands of English soldiers. Llywelyn, 'the brave, the great, the good', is presented both as a Christ-like figure and as a tragic hero whose only flaw is to trust not wisely but too well 'the friend [he] love[s]' who, Judas-like, betrays him for money. The 'Lamentation' itself occupies the final section of the poem, its ten lines possessing an emotional force and fluency which the rest of the poem lacks:

> Thy day of glory, hapless land, is o'er,
> Freedom will smile on Cambria no more.
> Hushed be the note of joy, the lively strain,
> Our King is fall'n, our prince, our father slain.
> Oh! Cambria mourn, dear hapless country mourn,
> Our prince is dead, our liberty is gone.
> Join all ye mountains, and ye streamlets too,
> As still your circling courses you pursue.
> Oh! mourn with me, but mourn alas in vain,
> Our country's freedom gone, our hero slain.

One of the most influential poems of the mid-eighteenth century, with which Williams would certainly have been familiar, was Gray's ode 'The Bard', in which the last bard left alive, after Edward I's conquest of Wales and the king's subsequent command to kill every member of the bardic order, defies the English pursuers who would kill him too; after comprehensively cursing Edward and every later English monarch, he hurls himself to his death from the crags high above the river Conwy rather than fall into the hands of his enemies. Gray's poem is set in a time after the Edwardian conquest of Wales, when the Bard's resistance to English rule can be expressed only by verbal defiance and the determination that he, not his conquerors, will decide when and how he dies.

Williams's poem, by contrast, shows the moment when the war against Edward's forces was lost – the 'before', 'during' and 'after' of the turning-point – and this immediacy adds to the agonised sense of 'if only things could have been different'. It would be interesting to know whether, when she wrote 'A Welsh Bard's Lamentation', she knew the great elegy for Llywelyn ap Gruffudd by Gruffudd ap yr Ynad Coch (perhaps in translation). The last lines of Williams's poem have much in common with the Welsh elegy, which shows all creation and the natural world turned upside down by so great a rupture of the natural order as Llywelyn's death[42] – although certainly the poetic device of a landscape joining in the expression of the poet's emotions was well known in English poetry also. What makes Williams's poem particularly interesting is that because it is set at the moment when Welsh independence was lost, it is able to communicate a powerful sense that the secure and happy past has gone for ever, that the present is harsh and precarious and that the future will be even bleaker: that is, it expresses in a national context the emotions which poems like 'Lines on the Banks of the Llunvey' and 'Sink not, my soul" express at a personal level.

The contrast between 'A Welsh Bard's Lamentation' and 'Sink not, my soul' in particular suggests that when Williams reflected overtly on her situation after the loss of her home and financial and social status, her religious upbringing required her to frame it as a test of faith to which she would make the expected and long-internalised response; but that through a persona very different from her own – a man whose life experience was far from hers in every respect and who, if he had existed, would have lived more than five hundred years earlier – she was able to express openly her sense that her comfortable, secure and happy world had gone for ever, that the loss was permanent, that her present was unhappy and her prospects cheerless. She was able to use – it seems, entirely unconsciously – an event from Welsh history (and, perhaps, a model from Welsh literature) to express openly feelings which could not acceptably be expressed elsewhere.

The two hundred subscribers to *Miscellaneous Poems* bought 387 copies of the book; the size of the print-run is unknown, although optimism (and funds) may have permitted 450.[44] Williams's Preface presents her collection to the subscribers with the modesty expected of a young first-time author, asking that her 'youth and circumstances may be taken into consideration' and that 'her little production will be read and judged not with harsh criticism but with kind indulgence'; the friends and relatives who subscribed would have known very well the unfortunate 'circumstances' she and her family had experienced over the previous four years. It is very unlikely that the book brought her much money or attention, but it performed its most significant function merely by existing. By writing its Preface in the third person she was able to refer to herself as 'The Authoress'; the publication of *Miscellaneous Poems* meant that becoming a writer was no longer an aspiration to console her for the way she was forced to earn her living but that, at the age of eighteen, she had succeed in imposing her definition of herself on the difficulties and indignities of the deeply unpropitious circumstances in which fate had placed her.

Because so little information about Jane Williams's early life has survived it is impossible to say exactly when she left Pipton Cottage. By the mid-1830s, however, (and probably earlier) she had moved to a different part of Glasbury and was working as a lady's companion.

A constant element of Jane Williams's personal and authorial lives is a crossing and recrossing of boundaries and borders – between nations, between urban and rural life, between social classes and financial categories, between cultures and between languages – and a lady's companion was in exactly this liminal position. Although her precise duties varied with the needs, wishes and temperament of her employer, the companion typically combined the roles of personal assistant and private secretary, providing companionship as and when required. She would be expected to behave and dress as if she were (almost) of the same social class as her employer; but everyone – especially the companion herself – would be very aware that her status was much lower.[45]

Williams seems to have been lucky in her employer, Isabella Hughes, who lived in a less remote part of the parish of Glasbury than the Morgans, although still one that was sparsely populated; the 1821 census records that whereas the Radnorshire part of the parish of Glasbury had 728 inhabitants, the Breconshire part, where both the Morgans and Hughes lived, had only 152. Aberlunvey House, where Hughes had lived for many years, stands at the side of the main road from Brecon to Hay-on-Wye; it has a clear (and very attractive) view of the village of Glasbury itself across the river Llynfi. The house is larger, more imposing and more comfortable than Pipton Cottage, and William's life there seems also to have been more enjoyable and more comfortable.[46]

Isabella Hughes was an important figure in Glasbury, both in her own right and as her father's daughter. The Rev. John Hughes had been a major landowner as well as an Anglican clergyman, and Isabella had filled the traditional role of the unmarried daughter who stayed with her parents and ran the household after her mother's death. She was rich; when her father died in 1809 she inherited from him land in Glasbury and estates in Denbighshire and Shropshire as well as substantial holdings of government stock.[47] She had been one of the local 'great and good' who subscribed to *Miscellaneous Poems* in 1824 and later became a friend of Jane Williams's step-grandmother, Jane Marsh.[48]

Isabella Hughes seems to have encouraged – or at least, not discouraged – Williams's desire to compensate for the fact that her formal education had ended at fourteen. As well as the bequest of clothes which employers frequently left to female servants, Hughes also left Williams all her books except those which she had herself inherited from her father – which suggests that Williams had been given free access to them during Hughes's lifetime. Hughes also allowed Williams to copy the research notes and antiquarian documents which her father had collected (Williams kept them, and many years later used them in an article on the history of Glasbury; see Chapter 5[49]). And Isabella Hughes apparently permitted Williams to exchange letters with the Rev Thomas Price (Carnhuanawc), in an age when some employers would have frowned on their unmarried female servant writing to an unmarried man (even if the subject of their correspondence *was* early medieval Irish round-houses[50]). There is also evidence to suggest that Isabella Hughes furthered Williams's ambitions as a writer, although for her own ends.

In 1838 *Twenty Essays on the Practical Improvement of God's Providential Dispensation as Means of Moral Discipline to the Christian* was published anonymously in London; Williams included it in the 1871 list of her publications. To someone familiar with her writing, reading the first six essays is a disconcerting experience; in treatment of subjects, organisation of material and, especially, in style, they bear no resemblance whatsoever to the rest of her published work. Essays VII–XI have some similarities to her writing at the level of individual phrases, but not of content or organisation, while Essays XII–XX resemble the other essays in their content and organisation while bearing clear traces of Williams's hand in their style – but (in comparison with her other writings) a very subdued Jane Williams.

Detailed analysis of the essays has led me to the following conclusions: Williams did not write Essays I–VI; for Essays VII–XI she probably revised another writer's drafts; and she wrote up Essays XII–XX from the notes or summaries of the same other writer. (I explain my reasons for these views in Appendix 2.)

So: who was the other writer? At this distance in time, and with no primary sources to explain the discrepancies between the earlier and later essays in the collection, any answer has to be speculative, but the most likely candidate has already been mentioned: the Rev. John Hughes, the father of Williams's employer Isabella.

I suggest the following course of events: John Hughes planned *Twenty Essays*, chose their subjects, wrote Essays I–VI and drafted VII–XI but was only able to prepare notes or summaries for XII–XX before his death. Isabella inherited these drafts and notes and would have liked to give the world the benefit of her father's religious and moral guidance but was aware that six completed essays would not be enough for a publishable book; in addition, publishing only six would have destroyed his overall design of twenty. Years later she had as her companion Jane Williams, whom she, as a subscriber to *Miscellaneous Poems*, knew to be a published author and who, as a devout Anglican, was doctrinally sound from the standpoint of the daughter of an Anglican clergyman. For Isabella Hughes, asking Williams to complete the twenty essays was likely to be her best chance of seeing her father's work in print; while no publisher would have considered the book a commercial proposition, Isabella Hughes could easily afford to pay for its publication.

This scenario is supported by the appearance the following year of an anonymous pamphlet, *Brief Remarks on a Tract entitled 'A Call to the Converted'*, which Williams also included in the 1871 list of her published work. In contrast to *Twenty Essays*, her authorship of *Brief Remarks* is indisputable: the pamphlet has her linguistic fingerprints all over it. It was provoked by the tract *A Call to the Converted* by William George Lambert, a member of the Plymouth Brethren; Williams judged Lambert's tract to be illogical in its arguments and sloppy in its style ('It contains neither apt thoughts nor apt words') and her tactic was to pretend to be charitable to its poor misguided author ('We will attribute all the wilder parts of "A Call to the Converted" to mental error'[51]). However, she refused to overlook his mistakes of grammar and syntax, since he had been well educated and should have known better ('As regards the literary style of the composition it is a pity that any one who has studied the standard of our tongue . . . should express himself so ill'[52]). Sometimes he expressed himself so badly that no charitable explanation was possible: 'In one or two instances we have been tempted to think . . . that it was intentionally obscure; but in others . . . we confess it could result only from helpless impotence of expression."[53] Throughout her pamphlet she criticised Lambert's illogical arguments and sloppy English not as an equal but from a position of lofty authority – the same technique she used later in her response to the 1847 Blue Books.

No response from Lambert was likely, however; his tract appeared in 1831, while *Brief Remarks* was published in 1839. Rebuttals of tracts and pamphlets were usually published soon after the work to which they responded; certainly it would have been very unusual for Williams's *Brief Remarks* to have been written much later than a few months after the publication of Lambert's tract. Eight years later, when *Brief Remarks* was published, no reader was likely to remember enough of Lambert's arguments to know what Williams was attacking (indeed, Lambert himself might well have forgotten).

As a contribution to debate on his tract, publishing *Brief Remarks* in 1839 was pointless.

Its publication does, however, make sense as an expression of thanks from Isabella Hughes to Williams for the work which had enabled John Hughes's essays to be published. For Williams, to see in print a piece of work she had probably had in manuscript for years would have helped reassure her that she really was still a writer – and if she resented some of the constraints which working on *Twenty Essays* had imposed on her, *Brief Remarks* would also have given her the satisfaction of seeing her own original and entirely characteristic writing in print.

Isabella Hughes died in 1845. By far the greater part of what she left – the houses and lands in Glasbury, the estates in Denbighshire and Shropshire, and the large holdings of government stock – went to her relatives. However, she also remembered Williams in her will, and the legacy changed Williams's life for ever. In addition to her clothes and books, Isabella Hughes left Williams an income for life: £100 a year, enough for a single middle-class woman to live on (especially if Williams joined her mother and younger sisters in Talgarth and shared household expenses with them[54]). The effect of this bequest (and presumably its intention) was that Williams would not need to spend the rest of her life working for whatever employers fate sent her, having to accept whatever treatment they chose to give her and with little time to pursue her own interests; it gave her financial independence. From then on she could spend her time as she wanted: reading, studying and, above all, writing. She was thirty-nine years old, and at last she had the freedom to live the life she wanted.

2

Responses to the Blue Books

The legacy from Isabella Hughes was the first of two great strokes of luck for Williams in the first half of the 1840s; the second was that she met Augusta Hall – later Lady Hall, and later still Lady Llanover – and became her protégée. Together the two events transformed her cultural, social and financial situation, and opened up the possibilities of the literary career she had wanted since she was in her teens. She had had to wait for more than twenty years, but now that her time had come she made the most of it.

A patron like Hall, willing to provide useful contacts, publicity and (if needed) financial support, was invaluable, and could make the difference between an author's success or failure regardless of the quality of her or his writing. In earlier periods the relationship between patron and protégé had often been named explicitly as patronage; by the nineteenth century it was often called 'friendship', but worked on the same principles and was no less essential to a writer's success, as the literary careers of Anna Jameson and Louisa Stuart Costello demonstrate. Costello's comment on the importance of having a 'powerful friend' in the literary world shows both the necessity for such help and the way the role of the patron was regarded.[1]

As Costello also pointed out, the difficulty of acquiring a willing and influential patron was even greater for a woman writer than for a man – but even more important, since women were typically outside the masculine social and professional networks that enabled the early careers of many male writers.[2] A male patron might employ a male writer as his private secretary or (if they were both Anglicans and the writer was qualified) appoint him to a living within his gift; neither option was possible for a woman.[3] Further, any suggestion that a female writer was dependent on the influence or financial support of a male patron would immediately raise salacious questions about their relationship.[4] For many people a woman who wrote for publication was already demonstrating indifference to the rules of respectable female behaviour; and dependence on a male patron, especially by a single woman, could provoke rumours that she was a 'kept woman' in a sexual as well as a financial sense. Jameson made the most of the fact that she was married; Costello was careful to choose an Anglican clergyman – a guarantor of respectability – as her first and most enduring patron.[5]

For a woman writer a female patron was therefore particularly valuable. The subscription list of Williams's *Miscellaneous Poems* is headed by 'Right Honourable Viscountess Hereford, 6 copies' across the top of the two columns. Lady Hereford was not the most generous subscriber – five others also bought six copies, while four bought a dozen each – but her name's prominence suggests that she was being presented as Williams's patroness, lending the cachet of her social status and the respectability of a female patron to the first book of a teenager who otherwise only had friends and relations for support.

No other contacts between Williams and Lady Hereford have been recorded – and, indeed, they may never have met. The friendship and patronage of Augusta Hall, however, was of an entirely different kind; it lasted for many years and was crucial to Williams's career as a writer. If she had not met Hall, the trajectories both of Williams's life and her writing career would have been very different.

When they met, Hall was already a major figure in social, cultural and political circles in south Wales and London.[6] Her husband, Sir Benjamin Hall, was an M.P. and they spent much of the parliamentary year in London, where Hall used their connections with the metropolitan elite to raise the profile of Wales and Welsh culture, especially its music. She was a major patron of the *eisteddfodau* organised by the Cymreigyddion in Abergavenny, and supported the Welsh Manuscript Society. At the Cardiff *Eisteddfod* of 1834 she had won a prize for an essay on 'The Advantages resulting from the Preservation of the Welsh Language and National Costume of Wales' (published in 1836), and she also played a major part in codifying 'traditional' Welsh women's costume. She wore her own version of Welsh dress herself, at Llanover but also sometimes in London, and not only required the female staff at Llanover to follow her example but encouraged 'the surrounding poor' to do so by giving them Christmas gifts of appropriately Welsh-woven cloth. (This did not always work, however.)[7]

After inheriting the Llanover estate from her father she had had a new house built there (in the style of an Elizabethan manor house) especially to accommodate large gatherings of the cultural, social and intellectual elite;[8] members of her house parties included relatives, neighbours, scholars, writers and aristocrats with a wide range of interests. Among them were Lady Greenly, who competed at the Abergavenny *eisteddfodau* as 'Llwydlaes'; the Welsh historian and Celtic scholar the Rev. Thomas Price (Carnhuanawc); Arthur James Johnes, a judge who translated the poetry of Dafydd ap Gwilym; the poet the Rev. John Jones (Tegid), who proposed a new form of Welsh orthography; the historian Angharad Llwyd; Sir Charles Morgan of Tredegar; Lady Charlotte Guest who, after learning Welsh with Tegid, translated the *Mabinogion* into English; the composer Brinley Richards; the three Thomas brothers of Brecon (a sculptor, a sculptor and medallion carver, and an architect); Archdeacon John Williams of Cardigan; the novelist and reviewer Geraldine Jewsbury; the novelist and memoir-writer Sidney Owenson Lady Morgan; the explorer and Egyptologist Sir Gardner Wilkinson; and the poet and philologist D. Silvan Evans. Frequent guests from outside Britain included Celtic scholars such as Baron Bunsen (philologist, Prussian ambassador to the Court of St James and Hall's brother-in-law), Professors Carl Lepsius and Schultz, Dr Carl Meyer, and the Breton antiquarian, author and folk-tale collector Hervé de Villemarqué.[9]

As a frequent visitor to Llanover Court, Williams was able to discuss a wide range of subjects with Hall's other house guests and use the impressive Llanover library to widen and deepen her knowledge further. Access to a good library was often difficult for women writers, who had neither the credentials nor contacts for the libraries of Oxford and Cambridge colleges and were not permitted to use the British Library. For Williams, who had left school in her mid-teens, the libraries at Aberllunvey House and Llanover Court and discussions with Hall's house guests provided an informal higher education.

Spending weeks – sometimes months – as a guest at Llanover Court or at the Halls' London house at 9 Great Stanhope Street had many social and cultural advantages, but when combined with Williams's modest income it also presented problems. She needed to be appropriately dressed at all times – more formally than when living in Talgarth – but this cost money. Her solution was ingenious, but also labour-intensive.[10]

A letter to her aunt from Llanover Court shows that her capsule wardrobe included only three dresses (over-dresses, all black: two for day and the third for evenings and special occasions). She needed two blouses each day, one to wear with her day dress and the other after changing for dinner, but she could not afford enough blouses to have some in the wash, or drying or airing, while she wore others. Instead of blouses, therefore, she used detachable half-sleeves and a 'dickey', which she had to sew to the inner seams of the bodice and sleeves of the over-dress before each wearing, and unpick for washing afterwards; further, since fast dyes for commercial use had not yet been developed, she had also to unpick and re-sew the bands of black velvet ribbon on the cuffs each time (the cover picture shows her wearing this costume for special occasions). She was very interested in clothes and her letters describe the dresses of her fashionable acquaintances in great detail; the fact that she had to perform the daily drudgery of unpicking and resewing herself – a maid would have cost money – while surrounded by 'all the splendid wardrobes of my associates' (who had ladies' maids) was a constant reminder both of her modest income and her need to keep up appearances. And on a practical level, it required time and energy (at least an hour each day) which she would far rather have spent reading or writing: 'having no maid, the trivial cares of dress [to be ready] for half-past seven o'clock dinners consume more minutes than I would willingly give it.'[11] It was, however, part of the price for membership of the Llanover circle – a price that was emphatically worth paying.

The new horizons which Hall's patronage opened to Williams were cultural and social as well as intellectual. In London, Williams accompanied Augusta Hall to places which she would otherwise not have visited and which she very much enjoyed: art and photographic galleries to see daguerrotype portraits and chromo-lithographs, 'the Panorama of Constantinople in Piccadilly', Madame Tussaud's waxworks, guided tours of workshops to see wallpaper-making and collodion photographs, and visits to the British Museum to see the Elgin Marbles ('the finest things ever done by human hands'[12]). At times Hall treated her like an unpaid lady's companion, taking Williams on some social calls but not others (at Kensington Palace 'I sat in the chariot while Lady Hall made a long visit to the Duchess of Inverness'). Hall also used her to get rid of an unwelcome visitor ('Mrs Gwynne Holford was let in by mistake and I had to go and talk to her'); and when Williams had gone exhausted to her room to rest she was bullied into agreeing to go for a walk with Hall 'although I told her I was just dead already'.[13]

But there were compensations. Through Hall she met the novelist Bulwer Lytton, the poet Samuel Rogers, the 'wonderfully acute' mathematician Charles Babbage, the Middle East explorer and archaeologist Sir Austen Layard, the German linguist Georg Sauerwein, the Italian artist Spiridione Gambarella, and the Polish patriot Prince Adam Jerzy Czartoryski. She also met British MPs and government ministers, the Speaker of the House of Commons, the ambassadors of Prussia, Turkey and Belgium, attachés from the Danish and United States embassies, and a wide range of the British aristocracy from knights and baronets to dukes. While she found most of the aristocrats deeply unimpressive ('the greatest number are a very common sort of people though bearing high titles'), she had more respect for the 'very remarkable' high achievers she met at Llanover Court and Stanhope Street who, she noted proudly, treated her 'as at least their equal and often as their superior'. At one point, she told her aunt, she found herself wishing that her mother (her aunt's younger sister, who had died three years earlier) 'could have known the honour and estimation into which quiet self-cultivation has brought me'.[14] Williams's reading during her fallow years as a writer equipped her to join the Llanover circle when the opportunity came, and she seized the chance it offered; the result was that she was living a life which she might earlier have dreamed of, but could never have realistically expected. Socially, intellectually and culturally as well as geographically she had come a long way from her previous life in Glasbury and Talgarth.

Her next piece of writing was deeply influenced by her visits to Llanover Court (where it was done), the Llanover circle, and the Llanover library; the arrangements for its publication also show how Hall used her influence – and money – to enable Williams's writing to go to places it would not have reached on its own.

The previous half-century had seen many incidents of civil unrest in Wales, both in response to particular and local grievances (strikes, demonstrations against wage cuts, the activities of secret organisations like the Scotch Cattle and the Daughters of Rebecca) and in support of explicitly political aims (the Merthyr Rising of 1831 in favour of political unions, and the Newport Rising of 1839 in support of the Charter, which demanded universal male suffrage and parliamentary reform).[15] The Newport Rising had been organised efficiently in great secrecy, and some commentators attributed the inability of magistrates to establish networks of informers to the fact that 'the lower orders [spoke] almost universally a language unknown to the educated classes'.[16]

From the government's point of view, the answer to this dangerous disaffection was education – education to teach the Welsh working classes views and values more acceptable to the governing classes – but before planning any reforms it was necessary to carry out an inquiry into the present state of education in Wales, especially the provision for teaching English. In the words of the MP who formally proposed it, if the Welsh people 'had been acquainted with the English language and [had] proper instruction provided, instead of being as they now are, a prey to designing hypocrites with religion on their lips and wickedness in their hearts', the disaffection which had led to the Rising might never have developed.[17] The political purposes of the inquiry were obvious from the start.

The title page of the Blue Books of 1846–7 (y Llyfrau Gleision) states that the inquiry was to be made 'into the State of Education in the Principality of Wales, and especially into the means afforded to the Labouring Classes of acquiring a Knowledge of the English Language'.[18] The inquiry divided Wales into three: R. R. W. Lingen reported on Carmarthenshire, Glamorganshire and Pembrokeshire in Part I; J. C. Symons on Breconshire, Cardiganshire, Radnorshire and Monmouthshire in Part II; H. V. Johnson on 'North Wales' (i.e. the rest of the country) in Part III. Each Commissioner was provided with Welsh-speaking assistants; there were ten in all, five of whom were students at St David's College Lampeter (the training college for Welsh Anglican clergymen).

The three Commissioners were English, Anglicans, lawyers and members of the upper middle class; that they knew nothing of Wales, education in Wales, Welsh society, history, language or literature was seen as proof of their objectivity. The Memorandum of Guidance from Sir James Kay-Shuttleworth, secretary to the Committee of Council on Education, emphasised that the Commissioners were to be 'men whose experience will enable them to examine the whole question with impartiality',[19] and this impartiality was demonstrated by the use of tables to present their statistical data and the formal language in which the reports were written. This impression of scientific objectivity gave a particular force to the reports' conclusions – that with a few shining exceptions, Welsh schools and teachers were inadequate, and that the Welsh people were typically liars, cheats and thieves who neglected their personal hygiene and were sexually promiscuous. Further, the Commissioners frequently related these negative attributes to the prevalence in Wales of religious Nonconformity and the Welsh language.

The importance of the Commissioners' assessment of the Welsh working class's knowledge of English made their hostility to the

Welsh language particularly significant. Lingen considered that, for Welsh children, learning to use English instead of Welsh was 'the most important part of their education'; Symons attacked 'the evils of the Welsh language'; Johnson declared that 'the limited resources of [the] Welsh [language] led to the degraded social and moral condition of the poorer classes in every county in North Wales'.[20] Taken together, the Blue Books' criticisms of the Welsh people and their 'moral character', their religious affiliations, literature and language, constituted an open attack on Welsh national identity.

The Blue Books sparked outrage and a bitter sense of betrayal in Wales; the eighteen months after their publication produced a large number of books and articles which argued fiercely against the Commissioners' preconceptions, methods of investigation and conclusions. Williams's response was twofold: firstly, a pamphlet (*Artegall: or, Remarks on the Reports of the Commissioners of Inquiry into the State of Education in Wales*, 1848), which, by analysing the Blue Books in devastating and sardonic detail, undermined the negative image of Wales they presented; secondly, a novel (*Cambrian Tales*, its chapters published in London in *Ainsworth's Magazine*, 1849–50), which presented entirely positive images of Wales and the Welsh people. The Blue Books cast a long shadow: it is not surprising that they provoked such a strong, and double, response from Williams.

Williams's literary career gained many advantages from Hall's patronage, and the publication of *Artegall* is a prime example. Hall paid the pamphlet's printing costs and she, rather than Williams, dealt directly with its publisher, William Rees of Llandovery. Because she was paying, the pamphlet could be published quickly and exactly as it was written, without the need to make any changes required by a publisher's reader.[21]

More than forty letters on the pamphlet's publication from Hall to William Rees have survived. Hall's initial intention was for 1,000 expensively bound copies on high-quality paper, many of which (she dithered between 500 and 700) would be sent to opinion formers and people of influence in London ('Ministers of State, noblemen, MPs, reviewers and editors of newspapers') to draw their attention to the inaccuracies and unfairness of the Blue Books' conclusions and to encourage them to support changes in government education policy in Wales. *Artegall* was to be published anonymously, with a personal letter from Hall recommending the book sent with each of these copies. Her name would mean the influential recipients would be more likely to read it, while the inevitable rumours that she was the author would give it even more publicity; a book thought to be by the celebrated Lady Hall would create far more of a stir than the same book written by an author the opinion formers had never heard of.

Hall reluctantly agreed with Rees that a cheaper edition, using smaller type and lower quality paper, should be produced for the 'lower orders' and sold for 6d (she wanted to charge 6½d). It was the de luxe edition, however, that received her close attention; she chose its paper, its font (small Pica) and the precise degrees of the blackness of its ink and the blueness of its cover (this had to be both 'dark' and 'brilliant', which must have presented Rees with a challenge). Her impatience for immediate results runs through her letters, sometimes a sharp nudge ('I really shall go distracted if the Proofs do not come faster'), sometimes a direct order ('I shall expect the Proofs back by return') and sometimes approaching a threat ('Your Printers will find that [with me] they have neither a Mole nor a Sluggard to deal with and must look sharp'). Williams's response to this barrage of demands for immediate action is indicated in Hall's only direct reference to her in the letters: that Williams 'never can attend (she says) to two things at once'. Hall's implication is that she herself could, and did.

While the conflict between Hall's impatience and Williams's wish for thoroughness may have strained their relationship, Hall's support for *Artegall* was unwavering. She declared to Rees that 'the more you read this work, the more you will see to admire in it – if ever a book was sold for its merits this must go like wild fire', and praised its readability: 'I would not have believed that so dry as well as so odious a subject could have been treated in a manner which renders the perusal of these pages intensely interesting to the most indifferent observer.' The pamphlet's arguments chimed with her own aim of raising Welsh national consciousness; she saw it as 'fresh capital for the national cause'. Williams's interests as a writer coincided with the interests of her enabling patron.

The attacks from Wales on the Blue Books were as varied as their authors, from the solidly constructed arguments of Ieuan Gwynedd that the Commissioners were irremediably prejudiced against 'our venerable language and our blessed religion' to the cheerful invective of Owen Owen Roberts, to whom the Anglican clergy in Wales were 'a cringing, sneaking, low-bred, servile, backbiting set who would make mischief between a Cow and a Haystack.[22] The London men of influence who received copies of *Artegall* from Hall could dismiss these responses as the result of the hurt pride of Welshmen who took the Blue Books' criticisms personally; *Artegall*, however, was different.

Williams's pamphlet was aimed directly at the London opinion formers, to convince them to support a change of policy. Her approach was to present herself as one of them: to make it clear that, unlike other commentators from Wales whom they might consider partisan, she was an impartial observer who was equally knowledgeable about the language, literature, history and culture of both Wales and England. She could therefore be trusted by metropolitan English readers to analyse accurately Welsh society, culture and education, and to identify the Reports' factual errors, inadequate methodology, and blatant prejudice. Throughout *Artegall* she emphasised that she shared the literary and educational background of her intended readership, from its title (one of the less prominent characters in Spenser's *Faerie Queene)* to its references to great names of English literature (Dryden, Pope, Johnson and Gray) and the eighteenth-century grammarian Lindley Murray. In all senses, she knew where her readers were coming from.

Her attack on the Blue Books was framed in explicitly moral terms; the epigraph to the pamphlet, from Book V of *The Faerie Queene*, explained her choice of title:

> Now take the right likewise, said Artegall,
> And counterpoise the same with so much wrong.

Her verdict was clear: the Commissioners' views of Wales and the Welsh people were not only factually inaccurate but 'at once illogical and unfair', and she (Artegall) was not merely pointing out their factual errors but defending the Welsh people against their moral slurs.

The first paragraph of *Artegall* made clear the moral dimension of this defence:

> The Reports of the Commissioners of Inquiry into the State of Education in Wales have done the people of that country a double wrong. They have traduced their national character, and in so doing, they have threatened an infringement upon their manifest social rights, their dearest existing interests, comprised in their ordinary modes of worship and instruction, their local customs, and their mother tongue.[23]

This charge against the Commissioners was direct and explicit: they had libelled the Welsh people as a nation, and had attacked and attempted to suppress Welsh religious practices, traditional culture and language. And since no reader was likely to opt for 'the wrong' over 'the right' (however those terms were defined in context) Williams's choice of language made any support for the Commissioners and their conclusions impossible from the outset (especially when these general moral terms were reinforced by emotive vocabulary such as 'traduced' and 'threatened an infringement upon their manifest . . . rights').

And if readers wondered *why* the Commissioners had chosen to wrong the Welsh people in this way, the pamphlet's third sentence provided a reason: 'The Commissioners were sent forth with instructions to make a case, and they have diligently and faithfully laboured to accomplish it.'[24] The accusation was clear: the Commissioners had been told their conclusions in advance, and they had dutifully followed orders – so that, far from being conducted with rigorous impartiality, the inquiry had been carried out as part of the British government's strategy to gain control of educational provision in Wales, and to further 'the direct and unprecedented interference of the Executive Government in the regular management and inspection of Schools . . . [which demands] Preventive Opposition from the watchful Friends of British Liberty'.[25] The Blue Books' conclusions and consequences therefore had far wider implications than educational provision in Wales alone; *Artegall* argued that they represented an attempt by the government to curtail the freedom of the British people.

The pamphlet did this by a series of accusations: that the Commissioners relied on evidence from unreliable informants 'whose ill will, inexperience, ignorance or prejudice rendered them incompetent'; that they presented conclusions which contradicted their own evidence; and that their comments on the Welsh language were both prejudiced and ill informed. Commissioner Symons had criticised Welsh schoolchildren for not replying immediately in fluent English when he made unexpected visits to schools and subjected the pupils to 'exhaustive examinations'; Williams pointed out that English was a foreign language to many Welsh schoolchildren, and suggested caustically that similarly unexpected visits to 'English boarding schools to carry out examination upon all the various topics of instruction. . .in French' would produce equally uncertain and ungrammatical replies. She compared the attempt to impose English on the Welsh people to the Normans' attempts to force their language on 'the depressed and despised Saxon' after the Norman Conquest, adding triumphantly: 'They tried various means to effect it and they failed.'[26]

If *Artegall* had only drawn attention to the inaccuracies and prejudice behind the Blue Books, it would merely have been one protest among many others (Ieuan Gwynedd, in particular, pointed out the inaccuracy of many of the Commissioners' figures). Williams's pamphlet, however, demonstrates two additional characteristics which give it an individual flavour. The first is the unashamed vigour of her attack; she described the evidence of one witness as 'disgusting' and said that evidence from others was 'so incompetent [that it] ought never to have obtained a place [even] in the Index'. Her judgement on a passage by Symons in Part II which began 'The Welsh language is a vast drawback to Wales . . .' and ended 'There is no Welsh literature worthy of the name' was a dismissive 'This is such manifest tirade as scarcely to deserve a comment.' She described a long, vague and structurally confused sentence by Lingen as 'read[ing] very much like *nonsense*', and damned another passage as 'one of the most feeble in structure and indistinct in expression that ever reflected the form of a vague and cloudy thought'.[27] She attacked not only the accuracy and fairness of the Commissioners' judgements but the language in which they were expressed, and *Artegall* includes a section which savages the Commissioners' language.

Their command of English was 'pitiable', she declared, pointing out that while they recorded 'the slightest inaccuracy in the English phraseology [of schoolteachers] and mark[ed] it with contempt', their own English was appalling; their grammar was so poor, she said, that 'a set of exercises on grammatical errors might indeed be compiled from the writings of the Commissioners for the cautionary use of Welshmen studying the English language'. She demonstrated this by quoting the grammatical rules of recognised authorities and then listing the ways the Commissioners flouted them: for example, lack of agreement between noun and verb, describing a place by an adjective applied correctly only to people, and using a verb which required a definite human subject with an abstract noun. Many of the examples that she subjected to particularly withering analysis were taken from Part II, for which Symons was responsible, and her conclusions on his use of English are reminiscent of the response of a weary school teacher to the depressingly inadequate written work of a particularly unintelligent pupil: until Symons 'attains a more creditable knowledge of etymology and syntax, we would earnestly recommend him to abstain from the use of metaphors and from all figures of speech'.[28]

As these examples show, the second of her major weapons of attack was mockery. She mocked the Commissioners' complacency in the rightness of their own conclusions, their illogicality and their habit of condemning the Welsh people for things they had not done but which the Commissioners thought they might possibly do in circumstances which did not actually exist. She also turned their own words against them, for example mocking the ridiculous grounds on which they found fault with Welsh schools: 'Everything is wrong in their eyes; even the Infant Schools are *"too exclusively infantine"*.'[29] Her immediate point – that to criticise an infants' school for being a school for infants was not merely 'illogical and unfair' but ludicrously so – gains its effect from the way she uses a direct quotation from the Blue Books themselves as evidence that the Commissioners were not only prejudiced but intellectually inadequate for their task.

These sweepingly magisterial criticisms show more than a willingness to challenge the authority of an official report; they also communicate a sense of Williams's enjoyment of destructive criticism. *Artegall*'s verdict on the Blue Books was doubly damning: not only had the Commissioners committed a moral wrong, they had done so in ungrammatical English. They therefore fully deserved the treatment she gave them: contempt for the way they had wronged Wales and the Welsh people, and mockery of their deplorable English.

In the early chapters of *Artegall* Williams drew on her personal knowledge and experience to illustrate the Commissioners' lack of knowledge and experience which had led them into error. She used her own 'more than twenty years['] experience of the Moral and Physical Condition of the [Welsh] People' to contradict Symons and Lingen when they said that the Welsh lived with their pigs and poultry, that girls had 'more leisure' than boys to attend school, and that girls' knowledge of domestic tasks was 'picked up' in their 'common routine of agricultural employment'. 'These gentlemen', she wrote sternly, 'cannot realise the necessities of rustic life.'[30] Her readers were left in no doubt that she did.

In the fifth chapter (of ten), however, she moved from the position of a knowledgeable observer of the Welsh and their practices to a position of open sympathy with them. When Symons ridiculed a woman who sent her children to school in turn because she could not afford to pay for them all to attend at the same time, she castigated him for 'sneer[ing] at the poor mother who boasted of sending her four children in quarterly turns to give equal advantage to each'.[31] Her sentence implies that she understood how the family's poverty prevented all four children being sent to school at the same time, while respecting the 'poor mother' for her wish to do as much for them as her limited resources allowed. Here Williams used the fact that 'poor' can both mean 'having very little money' and also function as an expression of pity; a neutral description of the mother's financial situation thus modulates into a sympathetic understanding of her motives, and Williams's choice of 'sneer' to describe Symons's attitude puts her firmly on the side of the Welsh mother.

This sympathetic understanding of the way Welsh people and their communities worked is shown even more clearly in a later chapter when Williams discusses their desire for education. After quoting several examples of this from the Reports, she comments:

> A [previously-mentioned] Welsh teacher told his pupils that 'not to faint' meant 'not to be daunted, not to give up'; and Welsh children do indeed exhibit a practical illustration of such words. Through all weathers, in winter's cold and summer's heat, through rain and wind, hail and snow, and thunder and lightning, crossing flooded brooks and rivers, by an unrailed plank, through roads which the Commissioners compare to ditches, along the faintly marked *rhiw* of the dreary and steep mountain wastes, over precipitous cliffs, which the Commissioners consider would be *'highly dangerous for English children'*, these ardent little creatures come, fearlessly and cheerfully, for miles to their schools.[32]

The choice of words in the second sentence emphasises the difficulties of the children's journey ('flooded', 'unrailed', 'dreary and steep', 'precipitous', 'dangerous'), and its structure mirrors the stages of their journey; the increasing length of the phrases creates an impetus which carries the reader along as if travelling across the same difficult and dangerous terrain as the children, and its final word – 'schools' – represents the end-goal both of the children's journey and the sentence. Her readers were being led to identify with the children on their difficult and dangerous journey, not with the Commissioners who looked down on them.

At the beginning of *Artegall* Williams had presented herself as an objective and knowledgeable observer who invited her readers to judge impartially the information she put before them; in the second half of the pamphlet she moved to a position which made it impossible for them not to sympathise with the 'poor' Welsh mother and the children 'ardent' for education. By this point she had crossed another border: in *Artegall*'s opening paragraph she had been an impartial authority on Wales and the Welsh people, but her demonstration of the illogicality and unfairness of the Commissioners' criticisms had led her to a point when she was so deeply embedded in the attitudes and priorities of Welsh rural society that she understood and sympathised with its members, and she described this in language which made it impossible for her readers not to understand and sympathise with them also.

Many responses to *Artegall* in both Welsh and English newspapers and periodicals were favourable; some were enthusiastic. Those which were not included a pamphlet by the bishop of St David's, Connop Thirlwall, accusing her of intellectual dishonesty in her attacks on the Commissioners.[33] This annoyed her enough to provoke a lengthy public reply in which she used the same methods as in *Artegall*, demonstrating that the bishop's sloppy use of language made his argument difficult to follow, but arguing that, where it was possible to understand his morass of verbiage, his arguments were both illogical and unfounded. In this riposte Williams made explicit both why she had written *Artegall* ('for the love of Wales') and the crux of her criticism of the Commissioners: 'The impression of the Welsh nation which was universally received from [the Blue Books] was that of heathen ignorance and [moral] impurity. The impression of the Welsh nation conveyed by *Artegall* is one of pervading piety and peace.'[34] Confident that her cause was right, she took on not only the Commissioners, who had the authority of the government behind them, but also the bishop – a highly-respected theological scholar and historian of Classical Greece, who learned enough Welsh to preach and conduct services in the language – and who was, moreover, a friend of Baron Bunsen. Like Artegall, she was prepared to fight powerful enemies.[35]

Figure 1. 'Artegall, or Whipping the Boys'
(cartoon by Hugh Hughes)

One of the most revealing responses in Wales to *Artegall,* and to Williams as its author, was not in words but an image: a cartoon by the artist Hugh Hughes. In 1848 he published nine cartoons on the Blue Books, in a series entitled *Pictures for the Millions of Wales.* By this time the name (though apparently nothing more) of *Artegall*'s author was known, and the last cartoon in the series was entitled 'Artegall, or Whipping the Boys'.[36] Its starting-point was Williams's tone in much of the pamphlet: the response of a weary school teacher to particularly backward pupils. The cartoon shows the three Commissioners (wearing wigs to show they are barristers) as naughty boys bawling in anticipation of the whipping they are about to receive from their teacher's large and fearsome birch. The cartoon is accompanied by Welsh and English texts; the Welsh text explains the significance of *Artegall* and the Blue Books to monoglot Welsh readers, whereas the English text assumes that its readers knew about both.

Both texts are written as monologues by Miss Jane Williams as she prepares to whip the Commissioners (who interject 'Oh please, no, Miss, we'll never do it again'), but the tone of the Welsh text is notably harsher. In the English text Miss Williams politely regrets the necessity of whipping the boys, while in the Welsh version she threatens to flog them so unmercifully that her birch will be worn down to its stump; and the insults in the Welsh version are considerably stronger. The Welsh version, unlike the English, sentences the Commissioners to punishment for their sins; two of them are to be exiled for life to England or Radnorshire, while the third gets hard labour in Llangollen where he must try – in vain – to learn Welsh.

In both texts, Hughes's warm approval for *Artegall* and its author is clear; the Welsh version refers to her as 'a patriotic lady' ('boneddiges wlatgarol') for her defence of the Welsh people. In choosing how to depict its author, however, Hughes faced a dilemma. Like most cartoonists of the period, he used a limited range of female stereotypes: the innocent young girl, the happy wife and mother, the virago, the grand lady, the old crone and so on. The stereotype of the schoolmistress (the obvious choice for *Artegall*) was sour-faced, flat-chested and graceless – a figure of fun, and certainly not someone to be taken seriously. But the author of a detailed and methodical dissection of official government reports, whose analysis was both intellectually impressive and patriotic, *had* to be taken seriously; Miss Jane Williams did not fit any of his stereotypes. The result is an uneasy hybrid. The cartoon Miss Williams shows some traces of the stereotypical features of a schoolmistress (the thin face and receding chin) but the hairstyle, dress and body are those of the sort of young woman who would typically be told not to worry her pretty little head about boring old government reports – and who, like the school mistress, would not be taken seriously. Hughes fully supported *Artegall*'s demolition of the Blue Books, but its author – because she was a woman who had demonstrated breadth of knowledge, literary skill, intellectual heft and the confidence to mock government-appointed Commissioners – did not fit any of his visual stereotypes. He admired Williams's writing, but at another level he did not know what to do with her.

Hughes's confusion over how to deal with Williams's authorship of *Artegall* is understandable; as the work of a woman in the 1840s who was previously unknown to the reading public, the assurance, authority and vigour of the pamphlet are remarkable. Williams gained her confidence from the fact that she was not merely expressing her own damning verdict on the Blue Books, but was doing so on behalf of the Welsh people. She was using her talent as a writer in the service of a cause greater than herself – to defend those who could not defend themselves in terms their accusers would recognise – and at the same time enjoying herself enormously.

Artegall remains an entertaining and invigorating read, and one of the most interesting and important pieces of political writing by a woman in Wales in the nineteenth century. Williams's authorship soon became generally known, and established her name as a writer; years later, her books still identified her on their title pages as 'Author of *Artegall*'. Her second response to the Blue Books, however, had a much more muted reception and she apparently did not make her authorship widely known.

The chapters of *Cambrian Tales* appeared anonymously between March 1849 and February 1850 in the London periodical *Ainsworth's Magazine*[37] (it was not published in book form, which suggests that it did not find enthusiastic readers; Williams claimed authorship in the 1871 list of her publications). Hall's letters to William Rees show that *Artegall* was written between late 1847 and early 1848, and published in March 1848. The publication dates, and the amount of work required for *Cambrian Tales*, suggest that Williams began at least to plan, and probably to write, her response in fiction to the Blue Books soon after the publication of her non-fictional analysis. In *Artegall* she attacked the Commissioners' negative images of Wales and the Welsh people in relation to their cleanliness, honesty, courtesy and the importance to them of education, their language and its literature; in *Cambrian Tales* she presented positive images of Wales and the Welsh people in relation to the same subjects. As with *Artegall*, *Cambrian Tales* shows her writing with a serious purpose – to defend the Welsh people from unfair criticism – while amusing herself by mocking those she thought deserved it. In *Artegall*, however, she had the text of the Blue Books – a single subject – to concentrate on; in *Cambrian Tales* she tried to weave together more, and more diverse, strands than her inexperience as a novelist allowed, and the plot and structure suffer accordingly, while its facility for mockery fades as it approaches its conclusion.

Cambrian Tales are set in and around Nantmawr, the country house in south-east Wales of Lady Jefferys, whose guests include her Welsh relatives and neighbours, and her English visitors. In the opening pages one of these visitors, Mr Willoughby, asks that Lady Jefferys's 'indigenous' guests should give 'some little insight into the character and habits of the people around us' for the benefit of 'lately arrived strangers' like him, and each of the twelve chapters focuses on a different aspect of Wales, the Welsh people, and Welsh life and culture.[38] The subjects are an eclectic mixture: the experiences of a Welsh parson, places of interest in the area (Llyn Safaddan, Mynydd Du, the ruins of Llanthony Abbey, a spectacular waterfall), Welsh legends and superstitions, the life of a Welsh gypsy, a Calvinist Methodist Sunday school, Welsh plant life (especially mosses and lichens), a Welsh country funeral, the history of Llywelyn ap Gruffudd, coracle fishing, the legend of Vortigern, Welsh agriculture and ancient monuments, the merits of the people of Cardiganshire, the custom of 'bidding' to weddings, idioms from English taken into Welsh and the hospitable instincts of Welsh farmers' wives.

Williams uses the country house party setting as a framework for these topics – although the framework is sometimes discarded. Chapters 3 and 4 (respectively on Welsh fairies and apparitions, and on giants) are presented as essays composed by one of the characters and read aloud to the others 'for their entertainment', while Chapter 5 consists of a letter from one of the English guests to his wife. Several of the chapters include poems; some of these are based on sources acknowledged in footnotes, but twelve, attributed to three different members of the house party, are by Williams (three of these were later reprinted in her volume *Celtic Fables*).[39] As this suggests, Williams's approach is very literary – quotations from Shakespeare, Spenser, Vaughan, Southey, Gray and Dryden's translation of Ovid are used either within the text or as epigraphs – and the image of Wales which emerges is rural, nostalgic and frequently antiquarian. The coal mines, foundries and steel works, and the cramped, unhealthy living conditions of industrial south Wales of the period are as far away as the political and social discontent exemplified by the Chartist rising and the Rebecca Riots.

The Welsh country house had been used before as a setting in which English visitors to the Welsh countryside discussed important topics (for example, Peacock's *Headlong Hall*, published in 1826), and the late 1840s had seen the publication of other books by women from England which used a mixture of factual accounts and fictional storylines to show Wales and Welsh people to English readers, *Sketches of Wales and the Welsh* by 'Amy' (1847) and *Traits and Stories of the Welsh Peasantry* by Anne Beale (1849) among them. *Traits and Stories* provides a particularly useful comparison with *Cambrian Tales*; both were published in 1849, both have the purpose of describing the Welsh to the English (*Traits and Stories* is 'an attempt at portraying [Welsh] persons and things truthfully'),[40] both fulfil this purpose by a mixture of factual essays and a fictional plot, and both are the work of women who had moved from England to live in Wales.

A comparison of the two books makes clear how Jane Williams played to her strengths, setting her fiction in a social milieu she was familiar with and creating characters whose preoccupations and foibles mirrored those of people she had met in that milieu (this may well have been deliberate; in an informal description of a novel she had recently read, she remarked, 'how silly clever people appear when they venture beyond the boundaries of their particular talents'[41]). By contrast, Anne Beale – whose social origins and occupation as a governess locate her among the English lower middle classes – set her plot among a social group to whom she was very much an outsider: the Welsh-speaking peasantry, as her title indicates. This was a world foreign to her in both social class and language, and one which she was unable to enter as an equal (a deficiency which elements of her plot and dialogue reveal all too cruelly).

By contrast, Nantmawr, the setting for *Cambrian Tales*, is clearly close to Llanover Court in its geographical location, its architecture and its mistress. Lady Jefferys is not a direct portrait of Augusta Hall – the fictional Lady is apparently an elderly childless widow, while Hall's husband and daughter were frequently in attendance at Llanover – but they share a love of music and taste in architecture. Nantmawr contains a 'veritable Elizabethan drawing-room', an obvious reference to the style Hall had chosen for Llanover Court;[42] Williams's use of 'veritable' makes it clear that the Elizabethan element was an imitation rather than the real thing, while the anachronism of an Elizabethan drawing-room carries its own comic weight. Certainly some of Lady Jefferys's remarks and reactions are similar to Hall's: Lady Jefferys slaps down an archdeacon's incautious generalisation, and she is certain she knows exactly how the pokers and shovel were arranged on a particular farmhouse hearth the previous day even though she did not see them herself.[43]

She is not the only member of the Llanover circle to be re-imagined. One of the guests is described in terms which immediately suggest the Welsh historian and Celtic scholar the Rev. Thomas Price of Cwmdu (Carnhuanawc) ('a middle-aged, middle-sized man with vivid eyes and dressed in an ill-cut black suit, still sat twanging the strings of a triple harp') and the life story of the Welsh curate shares enough features of Carnhuanawc's life to suggest a resemblance – but also enough differences to avoid presenting a literal portrait of him.[44]

Other characters are presented as figures of social comedy. Captain Harold, bored by an academic book on Middle Eastern archaeology ('Layard's *Monuments of* Nineveh'), indulges in 'charming episodes of personal contemplation in an adjacent mirror', while 'a stiff, stout little man . . . tak[es] shelter in the shadow of a newspaper from the unthreatened danger of conversation'. As often in Williams's writing, the punch here lies in adjectives: in the same way that 'veritable' mocked the concept of an Elizabethan drawing-room, so 'charming' communicates Captain Harold's vanity, and 'unthreatened' makes it clear that the 'stiff, stout little man's' precautions against being drawn into conversation are completely unnecessary, because no one wants to talk to him.[45] (Williams's letters show a similar talent for succinct but vivid personal description: the novelist Edward Bulwer Lytton was 'a very tall, narrow man . . . Both his limbs and features look as if he had been artificially stretched', the Millman daughters 'are large and wear their hair in long dripping ringlets around their plain faces', while an attaché at the Danish Embassy 'would not make either a Hamlet or a Laertes, but might do for a Guildernstern'.[46])

The characters are not drawn with great subtlety – that, clearly, was not the intention – and those from England are presented in a positive or negative light entirely in relation to their attitude to Wales; the attractive English characters are all sympathetic to Wales, while those who are scornful or contemptuous of the country and its people are presented negatively – and some are punished for it. Mrs Brown, who criticises Welsh legends as unrealistic and describes Welsh accents as 'horrid [and] provincial', is reduced to a state of catatonia by a horse ride across beautiful but 'precipitous' terrain, while Miss Fitzaymon, who mutters, 'How excessively rash and foolish these Welsh people are!', is moved to tears by the Welsh psalm sung at a village funeral ('so sweet, so simple and primitive'[47]). Later, however, she resumes her haughty attitude and is punished by nearly being thrown over a precipice by her bolting horse; she is saved from death, at risk of his own life, by the despised Welsh parson with the 'horrid' accent. When she has recovered she remains unrepentant, criticising the ruins of Llantony Abbey because they are 'not sufficiently covered with verdure, the scenery was dreary and unpromising and the flowers . . . were poor things, not worthy to be compared with those of the Alps'.[48]

While English characters are presented favourably or otherwise depending on their attitude to Wales, Welsh characters do not escape unscathed. Williams's mocking attitude to another guest at Nantmawr, Miss Dyddgu Perrot, is shown by her choice of verbs; Dyddgu 'stumped' down a steep slope, 'screamed' at lightning, and 'shrieked' with laughter at a bolting horse, and her noisy heartiness is a subject of considerable amusement.[49] Her preoccupation with the greatness of her own pedigree – a traditional reason for the English to mock the Welsh – is similarly ridiculed; she wants everyone to know that Sir Owen Rhys's grandfather and her own great-grandmother were brother and sister 'by the mother's side', and is 'piqued' at the thought that 'English people would not even perceive [this as a] near relationship'.[50] She is eccentric and clownishly hearty, but she is Welsh – and therefore (in the novel's scheme of things) essentially sympathetic, and her Welsh patriotism is never in doubt. The highest praise she can give the English Lady Edith is 'you deserve to be a Welshwoman.'[51]

Sir Owen Rhys, a local landowner whom the Nantmawr guests visit, is similarly presented; as a warm-hearted and eccentric squire he has very clear literary ancestors (Matthew Bramble in *Humphrey Clinker*, for example, and Squire Western in *Tom Jones*). He has the huntin', shootin' 'n' fishin' interests of the traditional country gentleman, and assumes that everyone is as interested in the achievements of 'his dear deceased dogs' and the flavour of Welsh mutton as he is. Like Dyddgu Perrot, he is patriotically Welsh; his highest praise for a brave and resourceful groom is that 'he has a true Welsh spirit in him'.[52]

Inasmuch as the novel has a plotline, it centres on the romance of Lady Edith Mortimer and Arthur Tudor; she had apparently refused his previous proposal of marriage, but at Nantmawr her newly sympathetic interest in Wales leads her to think again. He writes to ask if her feelings have changed; she drafts an encouraging reply. This happens in Chapter 7, and the conventions of fiction suggest that the novel will end with – at the very least – a sign that their futures lie together.

This, however, does not happen, and no further reference is made to their romance. Instead of suggesting that they will live happily ever after, the novel's last chapter consists of a poem on the scenery of the Wye, an example of a 'bidding' letter and a paean of praise from Lady Jefferys to the history and people of Cardiganshire ('The purest of Welsh dialects is spoken there', 'bright Aberystwyth' is 'the most cheerful of watering-places', and the people of Cardiganshire are 'remarkably acute and apt in learning, and bear a high character in all respects'[53]). The novel ends with a detailed description of Welsh lichens and mosses and a poem 'by' one of the characters (in fact by Williams) which declares that even if she had not had Welsh ancestors or read of glorious events in Welsh history or been enthralled by Welsh legends, the land of Wales alone would have been enough to 'enchain [her] heart'.[54] The need to cram into her last chapter as much favourable material about Wales as possible completely overcomes the demands of her plot.

The names of the characters are carefully chosen. 'Lady Edith Mortimer' has a Saxon first name (since 'Edith' was the name of King Harold's mistress it could suggest that she should end up with Captain Harold) and a surname which evokes the medieval Marcher lords, including the Mortimers who supported Edward I against Llywelyn ap Gruffydd. Arthur Tudor shares his name with Henry VII's eldest son; his first name carries the connotations of 'the once and future' king, his surname recalls the only Welsh dynasty to reign over both England and Wales. Their marriage, therefore, would present the joining in love of two nations, traditions and cultures, which had previously been enemies.

Other characters' names are equally resonant. Gwenllian, niece of Lady Jefferys, has the name of the daughter of Llywelyn ap Gruffydd and of the warrior queen of Deheubarth. Some Welsh names are specifically literary: 'Dyddgu' was a lover of the medieval poet Dafydd ap Gwilym and the subject of many of his poems; Britomart (Sir Owen's daughter) is a character in Spenser's *Faerie Queene*, while the parson Hugh Evans appears in *The Merry Wives of Windsor*. Miss Fitzaymon's surname evokes the medieval Norman lords who conquered Wales and held a similarly scornful view of the Welsh, while the artist Markwell, whose letter to his wife describes his detailed impressions of the Welsh, has an appropriate surname which recalls characters from Restoration comedy.

Markwell's letter makes clear Williams's purpose in writing *Cambrian Tales*: to counter the negative picture of Wales and the Welsh in the Blue Books. He writes as a first-time visitor to Wales, whose responses can therefore be seen as a counterpoint to those of the Commissioners (Lady Jefferys, by contrast, speaks about the Welsh from knowledge and experience). Markwell praises the Welsh people's 'remarkable yet unobtrusive self-respect', their benevolence, cleverness and courtesy – all of which contradicts the Commissioners' conclusions – and criticises the groups on whose evidence the Commissioners relied: the non-Welsh-speaking Anglican clergy, and those of the 'resident Welsh gentry . . . who ape[d] English customs' and required the services in the churches on their estates to be held in English.[55] His letter also contains a detailed description of the way Welsh had influenced the local variety of English.

Whereas Markwell's description of the Welsh contradicts the Blue Books explicitly, other passages do so by implication and relate closely to points Williams made in *Artegall*. References to the cleanliness and respectability of the farmhouse and its occupants in *Cambrian Tales* echo her defence of rural Welsh living arrangements in *Artegall*; Welsh children's determination to walk miles to school each day in *Cambrian Tales* mirrors her account in *Artegall* of the 'ardent little creatures' who walk cheerfully over 'steep mountain wastes [and] precipitous cliffs' to get an education; the decorous and earnest Bible study observed on a visit to a Sunday school in *Cambrian Tales* amplifies the account of religious education in *Artegall*; the description of negative government attitudes to the Welsh language in *Cambrian Tales*, which ignored the fact that 'Welsh is still the living language of Wales', summarises her remarks on government policy and the 'attachment' of the Welsh people to their language in *Artegall*; and the presentation of Welsh legends and folklore in *Cambrian Tales* is a more colourful riposte to the Commissioners' description of the Welsh as 'superstitious' than her counter-argument in *Artegall* (that the popularity of books on astrology in London showed that the English were equally superstitious).[56]

Cambrian Tales begins as a comedy of manners, with the apparent intention of using a conventional plotline (the romance of Lady Edith and Arthur Tudor) as the structure to which varied episodes and essays on aspects of Welsh life, culture and places could be attached. After the initial chapters, however, the plotline begins to fade before disappearing completely, and the seriousness of her intention – as in *Artegall*, to right the wrong done to the Welsh people in the Blue Books – overwhelms the comedic elements. Some of this can be attributed to the inexperience as a novelist which led her, for example, to create far more characters than she could handle efficiently (there are nineteen members of the house parties and their hosts, plus the farmer's family and assorted servants, shepherds and peasants). The primary cause, however, was her concern in *Cambrian Tales* to present an entirely positive picture of the Welsh people and every aspect of Welsh life and culture; each chapter begins with the motto CYMRU DROS BYTH! (glossed in a footnote as 'Wales for ever!'). Her ambition as a novelist was impressive, but the Welsh patriot in her overcame the writer.

Freed by Isabella Hughes's legacy from the need to find paid employment, and with her intellectual and literary interests stimulated by discussions with members of the Llanover circle and access to the Llanover library, Williams spent the two years from late 1847 to late 1849 in a burst of creativity sparked by the strength of her reactions to the Blue Books. It is perhaps not surprising that she did not later write anything comparable to *Artegall* – it would probably have needed the publication of another official document which she regarded as equally outrageous to provoke a similar response – but one can only speculate on her reason for not producing another novel. *Cambrian Tales* suggests that she was aware that her strengths in fiction lay in a comedy of manners set in a social milieu she knew well. However, for a writer who uses their own social circle as raw material, there are disadvantages in having a temperament that tends towards the satirical, especially if this extends to their patron (it would be interesting to know Hall's reaction to Lady Jefferys and her 'veritable Elizabethan drawing room', for example). Whatever the reasons, *Cambrian Tales* remained William's only attempt at fiction, and her next published works were all firmly rooted in real lives.

3

Varieties of Life Writing

While Williams's verbal portrait of Carnhuanawc in the Nantmawr drawing-room on the first page of *Cambrian Tales* reflected his importance in the Llanover circle, her later reference to him in the same chapter ('the lamented Carnhuanawc, the unambitious yet immortal Thomas Price of Cwmdu') is a tribute to the sense of personal and national loss felt at his death in November 1848.[1] Her next project, to collect and edit his essays and lectures, and to write his biography, was her first in a genre new to her, life writing, which occupied her for the next seven years, and all three of her works in this genre were written and published under the aegis of Augusta Hall. At Llanover Court, Hall attempted the modern recreation of a Welsh medieval noble household; while she did not copy her model so far as to appoint an official household poet, at this period Williams seems to have filled the unofficial role of household prose writer, putting her literary talents at the service of her patron.

Carnhuanawc had been well known through his popular history of Wales as well as his lectures and speeches on Welsh history and culture. He and Hall had been closely associated as founder-members of the Welsh Manuscript Society and through the Abergavenny Eisteddfodau; he was also one of the founders of the *Cambrian Quarterly Magazine* and was active in the work of the Welsh Minstrelsy Society. After his death there was a general sense that his achievements deserved the permanent memorial of a biography; he had no close relatives, and Hall seems to have appointed herself his literary executor, taking charge of his papers and choosing his biographer. Her first candidate was Archdeacon John Williams of Cardigan, who declined on the grounds that he was too busy (which may even have been true[2]). Williams was Hall's second choice.

The result was the *Literary Remains of the Rev. Thomas Price (Carnhuanawc)*. The first volume (1854) collected his most important essays, lectures and speeches; Williams's biography of him (1855) formed the second. Hall's involvement in the project was considerable; she owned the portrait of Carnhuanawc used for the frontispiece to Volume I, her niece and cousin had respectively taken and printed the photograph of him for the frontispiece of Volume II, and both volumes contained sketches made or copied by Hall, her daughter and her brother- and sister-in-law. Partly because of the cost of the illustrations, the volumes were published by subscription; around half the subscribers were clearly drawn from Hall's contacts book. These included British and foreign scholars and dignitaries: 'Her Majesty's Library', the Royal Library in Berlin, the Celtic scholars Dr Carl Meyer and Georg Sauerwein, academics, industrialists, London-based foreign diplomats, dukes and duchesses, the Speaker of the House of Commons and a dozen MPs, a lieutenant-general and (intriguingly) the rear admiral commanding the Pacific fleet. Welsh writers and intellectuals were also among the subscribers: the historian Angharad Llwyd, the translator of the *Mabinogion* Lady Charlotte Guest, the musician and folk song collector Maria Jane Williams (Llinos), the satirist David Owen (Brutus), the poet and lexicographer Daniel Silvan Evans, and the antiquary and literary scholar Thomas Stephens. There were also members of the Welsh reading public: a timber merchant from Brecon, a shoemaker from Crickhowell, a warehouseman from Abergavenny, an ironmonger from Nantyglo and a 'mechanic' (engineer) from Ebbw Vale.[3] Seven hundred copies of the book were printed, 516 of which were bought by 494 subscribers.

The result was that Williams was writing the biography for three distinct readerships: an international cultural and social elite (who might know little Welsh, if any); a Welsh intelligentsia knowledgeable about Welsh literature and culture; and a more general Welsh reading public who might have relatively little formal education but a deep and patriotic interest in Welsh history. For the first she needed to show that she was fully aware of contemporary views on the criteria for English biography to meet the expectations of the English (and Prussian, Belgian, Danish, Dutch and Turkish) subscribers, and that Carnhuanawc was not to be 'satirised as local and narrowly provincial'.[4] For the second she needed to demonstrate Carnhuanawc's deep and detailed research into Welsh history and literature. For the third she needed to emphasise not only his intellectual achievements but also his ardent patriotism, his defence of the Welsh language and the enthusiasm with which he promoted Welsh culture.

For the first of these readerships she was at pains to show that she was fully aware of the two tasks of the contemporary English biographer: to collect data and decide which to use and how best to use them. Her Preface to Volume II declared that 'the various particulars of information comprised in this Memoir have been carefully drawn from the most original and authentic authorities', and that her selection and ordering of them would show '[Carnhuanawc's] outward course of conduct and the inward tenor of his thought'. For the second of these readerships her Prefaces to both volumes emphasised that 'the political and literary history of the Cymry ever formed the central point . . . [of] all his antiquarian researches', with the aim of 'inform[ing] the world of things redounding to Cambria's national honour'. For the third group of readers she declared that 'Thomas Price was in all respects a true representative of his people', and reflected this by giving his biography the structure of a characteristically Welsh genre of the nineteenth century: the *cofiant*, which memorialised the life of a religious figure (*cofio* translates as 'to remember') whom readers were to take as an exemplar to guide and inspire their own actions.[5]

The *cofiant*'s pattern was well established: a brief account of the subject's (typically male) external life; his conversion and religious career; his final days and death; a portrait of him as Christian and minister; sermons preached at his funeral; his most notable sayings; and an elegy or elegies. If Williams's biography of Carnhuanawc is considered as presenting an exemplar not of religious devotion but of patriotism, it follows closely the typical structure of the *cofiant*.[6] By using this structure, Williams paid tribute to Carnhuanawc's status as a patriotic icon of Welsh-speaking Wales and demonstrated to the book's Welsh readers that she understood the literary as well as cultural tradition from which he came, and could memorialise him appropriately.

This is not to imply that her biography ignores Carnhuanawc's religious life and role. He was an Anglican clergyman, and the book makes clear his piety and good works, listing his charitable activities among his parishioners and offering an impressive and touching character reference: 'It is the uniform testimony of all who knew him from birth until his death that he was always good and always kind.'[7] It is rather that what made him exceptional – and therefore justified his biography – lay in his patriotism and the way he used his time and talents in the service of his country.

The events of his life can be briefly summarised. From a relatively poor, Welsh-speaking background he received a good education through his own and his family's financial sacrifices, became an Anglican clergyman, wrote essays and gave lectures on Welsh and Celtic history and literature, argued for the importance of the Welsh language to the Welsh people, supported *eisteddfodau* and many other Welsh cultural organisations and died, much respected and admired, at the age of sixty-one.

The biography's equivalent to the *cofiant*'s religious conversion occurred when he applied for a position as vicar on the West Indian island of St Vincent. The three parishes in Breconshire where he was a curate demanded much work for very little money (the absentee vicar kept most of the stipend and tithes); the parish in St Vincent offered £1,400 a year. His elder brother (his only surviving relative) and his friends were concerned for his health and begged him not to go, but he was adamant. He bought his tropical outfit, packed his trunks, made his final preparations – and then discovered that vagaries of the island's currency meant the nominal £1,400 would really be worth less than half its face value. He immediately decided not to go.[8]

No mitigating circumstances are offered, and in context his decisions first to go and then not to go to St Vincent seem entirely mercenary; at the age of thirty-two he was too old for the episode to be presented as a mere folly of impetuous youth. Williams presents it as the turning-point in his life: 'The impression left on Mr Price's mind by this occurrence seems to have been that he had erred in permitting any considerations to counter-balance his disinterested desire of devoting himself to the Welsh people.' After this she shows him involved in Welsh cultural activities and research until his brother's death six years later, after which '[t]he last close tie of family attachment having thus been dissevered, Mr Price became henceforth wholly the property of his country'. The biography then shows him becoming a writer and public speaker on Welsh and Celtic languages, literature and history; that is, it describes his 'conversion' to Welsh patriotism and then recounts his career as a patriot rather than a preacher.[9]

Carnhuanawc's lectures and speeches can be seen as taking the place of sermons in the traditional *cofiant*; they often used the same techniques of rhetorical questions and vivid metaphors. His response to English commentators' suggestions that the Welsh language should be eradicated was: 'If he who would destroy a light-house would be deemed a barbarian, what shall we say of the man who wishes to destroy a living language?', and a speech given the year after he began his patriotic career declared: 'I trust that as long as [our] mountains shall lift up their heads to the skies, this patriotic ardour of our nation will not cease to blaze as high as a bright and splendid beacon-fire.'[10]

The account of his last days and death also fits exactly the pattern of the *cofiant*. He attended the *eisteddfod* of Cymreigyddion y Fenni at Abergavenny, although clearly ill; in spite of his obvious weakness and 'the deadly pallor of his complexion and the excessive brightness of his eyes', he lectured on Welsh bards, the influence of Welsh traditions on European literature, and 'the national harp and the joy of its music'. During the following fortnight he became weaker, but continued to carry out his parish duties; when invited to Llanover Court he declined, telling the messengers that 'they might as well take a corpse with them in the carriage as take me'. A few days later, after his housekeeper's daughter had taken him his dinner she went to the adjoining room, 'sitting down there to her harp, as usual at his meal-times, and playing several times one of his favourite Welsh airs, "Syr Harri Ddu"'. When she went to check on him later she found him in a coma; he died without regaining consciousness several hours afterwards.[11]

The message was clear; Carnhuanawc had the perfect death for a Welsh patriot. To the end of his life he had exerted – indeed, overexerted – himself in the service of his country and accepted calmly his approaching death. Most fitting of all, the last thing he heard on earth was one of his favourite pieces of Welsh traditional music played on his favourite, and traditionally Welsh, instrument – and the words of the song were notably appropriate, since Syr Harri loved above all things his country, its language, and the songs of his ancestral harp.[12] Carnhuanawc's last days and death could hardly have been more exemplary.

In place of the *cofiant*'s funeral sermons and elegies, Williams includes a chapter entitled 'Testimonies to Carnhuanawc's Worth' (a collection of eulogies to his patriotism and his years spent preaching the importance of the Welsh language, literature and culture to the Welsh people) from friends, academics and admirers; she also includes the *englynion* entered in competition at the Tremadoc *Eisteddfod* in 1851 for an epitaph on him. As preachers memorialised in *cofiannau* were shown devoting their talents to spread the faith, so her biography shows Carnhuanawc using his gifts in the patriotic work of raising the status of Wales and extending knowledge of its literature, history and culture.

The *cofiant* frequently ends by suggesting that although its subject is dead, his influence and work remain. Williams ends her biography of Carnhuanawc by focusing on his lifelong interest in harp music – as a boy he had made his own harp – with quotations from his letters to illustrate his technical and musical knowledge. The chapter ends with a poem, 'Lines to the Welsh Harp', by Williams herself under her bardic name of 'Ysgafell', which presents the harp and its music not merely as one of Carnhuanawc's patriotic and cultural interests but as his surrogate, celebrating his country's history in music as he had done in words. Its final stanza draws inspiration from a historical source which would have been well known to her Welsh readers:

> The Cymry still a people shall remain,
> And hold wild Wales through good and ill secure,
> Their language they shall keep, their harp retain,
> The bards declare, while earth and time endure![13]

This is a versification of the words of the Old Man of Pencader when asked by Henry II in 1163 to predict the outcome of Henry's Welsh campaign: 'Whatever else may come to pass, I do not think that on the day of Direst Judgment any race other than the Welsh, or any other language, will give answer to the Supreme Judge of all for this small corner of the earth.'[14] This anecdote, taken from the *Description of Wales* by Giraldus Cambrensis, seems to have had a particular resonance for Williams (she also used it in *Artegall*); by placing it at the end of her work, like Giraldus, she implied, like him, that it was her definitive opinion on the subject. Williams's final stanza, therefore, asserted that Welsh identity, and the Welsh language and Welsh harp music, would also survive; like a *cofiant*, her biography of Carnhuanawc ends by declaring that the cause to which he had devoted his life would live on.

While her biography's affection and respect for Carnhuanawc are entirely serious, there is also occasional comic relief. A detailed list of Carnhuanawc's worthy but unexciting paternal ancestors is enlivened by the completely irrelevant information that one of them was 'renowned in memory for the maiden-like profusion and fineness of his hair', and an account of the boy Carnhuanawc looking at the night sky through 'a small spy-glass' shows him bathetically musing that if only he had owned 'a telescope such as Sir Isaac Newton had used' he would have been able to see the planet Saturn 'instead of merely getting a view of Llandrindod'.[15]

At times the humour verges on farce. After Carnhuanawc became well known he was plagued by unexpected and unwelcome visits from celebrity hunters at his rectory in Cwm Du; since his study was at the back of the house, when he heard 'an unusual noise of wheels or voices' at the front he would leave by the back door and 'take refuge on the Briannog mountain before the besiegers had asked if he was at home', so that his housekeeper could say truthfully that he was out. Some of his friends who knew this habit 'used to amuse themselves occasionally by making an attack at the front door and then rushing round to catch the master of the house plunging from the back door to his sylvan retreat'.[16] Williams's use of mock-heroic vocabulary ('take refuge', 'besiegers', 'making an attack', 'sylvan retreat') adds to the ridiculous picture of the distinguished scholar being caught sneaking out of the back door of his own house; it also makes the more serious point that he guarded his privacy and time.

There is little similar justification for the longest and most sustained example of comic relief, however: the inclusion of letters from Lady Hester Stanhope to Carnhuanawc's father in 1808–9. For several months Lady Hester rented houses in the Builth area, and in her letters (among Carnhuanawc's papers) treated his father as an unpaid agent-cum-servant and issued peremptory orders on preparations for her arrival: insisting that a door be created to connect two rooms in her lodgings, sending two sorts of green paint (with instructions for their use) as 'good paint cannot be got in the country I know', and demanding that her landlady grow vegetables for her. Her letters are unconsciously very entertaining, and it is easy to see why Williams thought they deserved readers, but their relevance to Carnhuanawc's life is marginal at best. Williams was clearly aware of this, admitting that their presence in the biography 'may critically be deemed a superfluous redundancy' but still including them; certainly they provide an entertaining interlude, but it is an interlude which (taking up the whole of one chapter) lasts far too long.[17]

Williams's biography of Carnhuanawc succeeds in paying tribute to his achievements as a historian, explaining the affection and respect in which he was held as a patriot, and communicating the gentleness, modesty and dedication of his character together with a sense of warmth towards him as a person; it shows admiration, respect and personal liking without falling into the trap of hagiography. It would have been interesting to see how Williams handled the challenge of another third-person biography, but when she next wrote someone's life story it was to be in the guise of an autobiography. Before then, however, came a brief dip into the waters of her own early life; the memories themselves were happy, but the effects of looking back to a time when her life had been very different were far more complicated.

The second of her three pieces of life writing, *The Origin, Rise and Progress of the Paper People* (1856), is the memoir of a game which Williams and her siblings devised and played in childhood. They created a miniature paper version of the society in which they lived, including institutions such as the Houses of Parliament, the Bank of England, law courts and government departments, as well as shops, houses, cities and farms and country estates. The only institution not mirrored in the paper world was the Church of England, because their mother thought it blasphemous to have a paper clergyman take a service from the Anglican Book of Common Prayer; the children decided that the Paper People would have to exist without the benefits of religion.[18]

The paper figures were very detailed. Paper army officers had 'high caps with feathers on their heads and swords in their hands'; paper children played with tiny paper dolls; paper travelling-shows charged customers paper money to see paper 'wild beasts and birds and reptiles'; paper families with paper servants gave elegant receptions with paper sirloins of beef, paper plum puddings and paper fruits and cakes in paper dining rooms equipped with paper cutlery and crockery, and pieces of red paper were fixed between the bars of paper grates to form a paper 'blazing fire'. The Paper People included the inhabitants of many different countries, and the obsessive attention to detail is remarkable.[19] As with Williams's biography of Carnhuanawc, Hall was responsible for the illustrations; in this case, her own painted sketches of Paper People (a soldier, Welsh woman, a Hindoo [*sic*], etc.) and a frontispiece which shows four small children (plus cat) playing with the paper figures under the benevolent supervision of a respectably dressed woman.

The fact that the Williams children chose to make a pedantically accurate miniature version of the world they lived in rather than creating something new and imaginatively different (as did the Brontë children, for example, in their tales of Gondal and Angria) suggests the power of their conventional upbringing; Williams explicitly refers to their 'desire to render the condition of the paper people conformable to existing realities'.[20] The conventionally named Paper Person Lord James Middleton stands in revealing contrast to the Brontës' exotic Duke of Zamorna, for example; and Lord James Middleton's 'strange unheard-of fate' is not some dramatically Gothic doom, but being handed to another family by mistake.[21]

Part I of the *Paper People* describes the origins of this paper world and Williams's two youngest brothers cutting out additional paper figures; their ages show that this happened just before her family lost its money and her world changed. It is a picture of a happy everyday domestic scene, unremarkable at the time but significant later as a reminder of what had been lost (and tellingly for a writer so critical of lapses in grammar, the sentence in which she describes this is verbless). It is not surprising that in Part II she describes looking through the chest which held all the Paper People (she was the family curator) as like 'a desolate visit to Herculaneum or Pompeii – a people and region transferred to death amidst the unfinished acts of everyday life'.[22] They had become the material relics of a period of her life which was now long past.

But then the Paper People exerted 'their old unbroken spell' and she was a child again, writing in the present tense: 'At Buckingham Palace household troops are on guard, and within is King Alfred the IVth, with the privy council in convocation . . ."[23] By the last paragraph, however, the adult was back in control, rationalising that the game made the children 'quiet, cheerful, and thoroughly contented', and taught them 'self-control' (given the disputes she had described between some of the paper figures – and therefore their handlers – this seems an unduly rose-coloured view). It is the memory of a happy, secure, materially comfortable childhood that is the real subject of the book; the details of the paper uniforms, cakes and cutlery are incidental.[24] Remembering the security and happiness of the time when she and her siblings had played the game, however, inevitably brought memories of its abrupt end – as she said, the 'acts of everyday life' the Paper People commemorated were 'unfinished'. She was aware that, in all senses, she could not go home again; but this thought inevitably raised the question: where now was home? Where did she belong?

Which makes her next move an intriguing one. By the time *The Paper People* was published, Williams had moved from Talgarth to Chelsea, where she lived for the rest of her life. At forty-nine she was living where she chose for the first time, and her reasons for the move are worth considering – especially since the move was a gamble, and she was not by nature a great gambler. The explanation she gave later to the Royal Literary Fund was that she needed 'to avoid the severity of winter among the Welsh mountains' because her 'fragile' health had 'broke[n] down'.[25] However, Talgarth is not situated 'among the Welsh mountains' and winters there are not particularly 'severe' (it typically shares the temperature patterns of nearby towns such as Brecon and Hay). It seems that Williams was offering a socially acceptable reason for the move and relying on the fund's trustees having a limited knowledge of Welsh geography. Further, the air quality in Chelsea was less than desirable for someone with a heart-lung condition who suffered from breathing difficulties, since it was the site of several industrial enterprises (a distillery, a white-lead factory, a waterworks which collected waste from sewers) which damaged air quality.[26]

Certainly, living in London rather than Talgarth had advantages for the new direction she planned for her writing: a project which began as a study of Felicia Hemans's poetry but which expanded to become a history of women's writing in English. Whereas *Artegall* and the *Literary Remains* of Carnhuanawc had been of particular interest to Welsh readers, this new project had a potential readership throughout the English-speaking world, and if successful might lead to new editions of the works of the authors featured in her book – and she would be the obvious editor. With this in mind, it made sense to base herself in London, where she could more easily be in contact with publishers, editors and reviewers in person rather than by post from Talgarth.

Living in London also gave her the option of keeping Augusta Hall and her own brother Edward at arm's length. Certainly she was happy to keep in touch with Hall, continuing to stay at Llanover Court (and use its library) when on the way back to London after visits to relatives in Talgarth and Hereford, and meeting in London when Hall was there; but when living in London she was no longer so completely at Hall's beck and call as she had been when staying with her. While she and Hall had been working towards the same end in the production of *Artegall* and the *Literary Remains* of Carnhuanawc, the new direction of Williams's writing meant that their interests were less closely aligned, and there were considerable differences of temperament between Hall – full of new projects and ideas which were all to be carried out immediately if not sooner – and Williams's more systematic, methodical approach, epitomised by her defensive remark to Hall that she could only do one thing at any one time. Williams had genuine respect and admiration for Hall and was flattered by her friendship and deeply grateful for all the opportunities – social, cultural, intellectual and practical – which Hall's patronage had given her, but at times she seems to have felt that a little of Augusta Hall went a very long way.

There is also evidence that she preferred to keep a distance between herself and Edward, the second of her three brothers and ten years her junior. Two of her letters show that Edward was determined to exploit her friendships with important and influential people for his own benefit and that she was equally determined to stop him. In a letter of 1851 to her aunt, written when she was staying in London with Hall, she described her 'dread of the use w[hic]h he might attempt to make' of the acquaintance if she introduced him to the Halls, explaining that 'his previous conduct' did not allow her 'to feel confidence in his gentlemanly and proper comportment'.[27] (To her aunt she clearly felt no need to expand on his lack of 'gentlemanly and proper comportment'; similar euphemisms often referred to the behaviour of a heavy drinker, and it may be relevant that Edward was later diagnosed as a chronic alcoholic.) And in a letter written to Arthur Johnes, a fellow member of the Llanover circle who was a judge on the north Wales circuit, she passed on a request from Edward that Johnes would pull strings to get Edward a job as registrar in a deftly worded letter which let Johnes know that she wanted him to do exactly nothing about it.[28]

After the death of Isabella Hughes in 1845, Williams had joined her mother and two youngest sisters at Neuadd Felen in Talgarth; after their mother died in 1851 Edward moved in, and on his marriage in June 1854 was joined by his wife Catherine[29] – who then replaced Jane as mistress of the house. When Jane and Edward were living separately it was easier to refuse to cooperate with him than when they were living under the same roof; moving to Chelsea solved a lot of problems. Another advantage was that Chelsea was well established as the home of writers and artists, both major – Leigh Hunt, Carlyle, Turner, Holman Hunt, Daniel Maclise (and, for a time, Karl Marx) – and minor, such as the authors Samuel Carter Hall, his wife Anna Maria, and Geraldine Jewsbury, whom Williams had met at Llanover (both women later wrote references for her to the Royal Literary Fund).[30] In Chelsea Williams was living among people with the same literary, artistic and intellectual interests as her own; it was also an area of respectable lodging houses suitable for a middle-class single woman on a modest income. She moved there planning that her next writing project would be an ambitious history of women's writing in English, and may have already started work on it. However, it seems that Augusta Hall had other ideas.

In 1851 Elizabeth Davis, a Welsh woman better known as Betsi Cadwaladr, worked at the Halls' London house as a temporary housemaid; Augusta Hall took a particular interest in her because she was not only Welsh-speaking but the daughter of the well-known preacher Dafydd Cadwaladr. The following year Betsi Cadwaladr worked for the Llanovers again, this time as the housekeeper-caretaker of one of their smaller houses in south Wales.[31] In the autumn of 1854, when Betsi Cadwaladr applied to become

Figure 2. Betsi Cadwaladr.

one of Florence Nightingale's nurses during the Crimean War, Hall gave her a character reference.[32] Cadwaladr returned to London from the Crimea in November 1855, with very little money and unable to work because of her 'broken health' (in the book's frontispiece she is deliberately posed to draw attention to her damaged right hand).[33] Servants in that situation often turned to their ex-employers, but most of Cadwaladr's were either dead, abroad or untraceable; Hall, who had taken a particular interest in her from the beginning and who had supported her joining Nightingale's nurses, was the obvious person to contact. Cadwaladr had led an interesting and adventurous life long before she went to the Crimea, and a book about her would both raise money for her and draw attention to the patriotic service of a remarkable Welsh woman – which would have pleased Hall. And if Cadwaladr herself could not produce a readable account, then Hall had a protégée who could. It is not known whether Hall paid the costs of publication, as she had with *Artegall;* Williams presumably gave her services free as her own contribution to help Cadwaladr.

Although Hall appears in *The Autobiography of Elizabeth Davis a Balaclava Nurse* only as 'Lady ________' she is clearly identifiable, and the fact that she permitted the use of her English translation of part of a Welsh poem by Cadwaladr's father shows that she knew in advance about the book and approved of it.[34] While there is no direct evidence that the book was Hall's idea, nothing about Cadwaladr's life and personality as revealed in the *Autobiography* suggests that she would have thought in terms of a book, while Williams's Preface to it contains so many complaints about her difficulties in assessing the accuracy of the information she received, her irritation at its inevitable factual mistakes and the fact that its composition had 'involved much care and labour . . . [and] trouble' that if the project had been her idea, it seems unlikely she would have completed it.[35] Her defensive resentment makes sense, however, if the book is seen as an interruption to her work on her history of women writers in English. However willing she was to give her skill and experience as a writer to help Cadwaladr, the longer she spent on the *Autobiography*, the longer it would be before she could finish the book in which she had invested so many hopes – not only of literary success, but of making some money.

It is one of the ironies of Jane Williams's literary afterlife that her best-known writing today is the book least typical of her work as a whole, and the one for which she has received least credit[36] – but then *The Autobiography of Elizabeth Davis a Balaclava Nurse* (1857) is itself an anomaly in several ways. It is not an autobiography, since it does not meet the essential definition of an autobiography that the person who lived the life wrote the book, and the book's subject is far better known – certainly in Wales – by another name. Further, autobiography was regarded by many Victorians as a border genre, neither history nor a novel but possessing some characteristics of both;[37] the distinctions between genres were blurred further by the fact that many novelists of the period, including

Dickens, the Brontës and Charles Kingsley, used autobiographical narration (the subtitle of *Jane Eyre*, for example, is *An Autobiography*). If autobiography is itself a border genre, Betsi Cadwaladr's *Autobiography*, situated on the border of a border genre, is even more liminal. And the fact that it told a woman's life story would have made its status even more dubious to many Victorian readers.[38]

In an age when the ideal model of Victorian femininity knew that her place was in the domestic sphere, a woman who allowed the story of her life to be published was putting herself before the public in a very undesirable way. Further, Cadwaladr's *Autobiography* presented her as having lived an independent life that was interesting in its own right rather than, for example, because she was a famous man's wife, daughter, sister or mistress. ('From their own constitution and from the station they occupy in the world [women are] strictly relative', wrote a popular – woman – writer of the period).[39] Betsi Cadwaladr's father Dafydd was a well-known preacher with the Countess of Huntingdon's Connection and a close friend of the prominent Calvinistic Methodist Thomas Charles of Bala, and her biography could well have been written as the life of a dutiful and admiring daughter; instead, it shows her flouting her father's paternal and spiritual authority (and winning the battle of wills between them) and making a life for herself many thousands of miles away from him. Other characters come and go in its pages, but she always remains the focus of the narrative's interest; indeed, the *Autobiography* shares many features of the picaresque novel, since it has an adventurous and solitary protagonist and an episodic structure, includes dramatic and frequently improbable incidents, has characters who appear, disappear and sometimes reappear by extraordinary coincidence, and lacks a tidy conclusion.[40]

Certainly Cadwaladr had led an action-packed life even before she volunteered to be one of Florence Nightingale's nurses, and the *Autobiography* shows her as a woman who was not merely self-reliant but self-sufficient (another reason for contemporaries to disapprove). It records her unhappiness at home after the death of her mother when she was five, her subsequent running away from the family farm outside Bala four years later to the house of her father's landlord in the town and how, five years later still, after promising to stay with her landlord's family for another year, 'a sudden thought occurred to me . . . that I must see something more of the world' – so she ran away to Liverpool.[41]

She then recounts how, after five years there as a domestic servant, travelling widely in Britain, Ireland and Europe with her employers, she ran away again – this time from a fiancé – to London, and later began working as maid to a series of captains' wives on merchant ships, visiting India, China, Brazil, Singapore, Greece, Mauritius, Australia, the West Indies, St Helena, South Africa, Egypt and islands in the Pacific, alternating these voyages with periods in Britain as a domestic servant; she also worked in wards at Guy's Hospital in London. Her first fiancé, whom she presents as the love of her life, drowned when his ship was wrecked as it approached Liverpool, two days before they were to be married; she broke off two other engagements, one because 'I resented indignantly his having said that he would be my master', the second after a quarrel because she had not told her sister of her engagement ('He wrote to me afterwards, and sent a friend to me to try and make it up again, but I refused to have any more to say to him'[42]). She rejected a persistent suitor who followed her halfway round the world and tried to kidnap her ('I was resolute to die rather than be married [to him]'), and more than twenty other proposals of marriage.[43]

In October 1854, after reading a newspaper account of the Battle of the Alma, she offered her services as a military nurse, in order 'to see what was going on and take care of the wounded' (her order of priorities is revealing), lying about her age.[44] Determined to go to Balaclava in the Crimea, and rejecting the authority of Florence Nightingale (whose official instructions restricted her activities to Turkey), she spent nine months working in the General (military) Hospital at Balaclava: six weeks as a nurse and the rest of the time as the cook in charge of the kitchen which provided special diets for soldiers too weak or ill to be able to stomach British Army rations. By her own account she worked a nineteen-hour day, seven days a week, and it is not surprising that her health gave way. Equally, it is not surprising that Hall might have thought that such an extraordinary life would make for a readable book which could raise money to help Cadwaladr in her poverty-stricken old age.

Williams's first task was to get the facts of Cadwaladr's life by interviewing her – in 1856, according to her Preface, in London. Unfortunately everything depended on Cadwaladr's memory, since she had no diaries, letters or other written records – and her memory had large gaps. While Cadwaladr gave an account of her life 'to the best of her recollection', Williams ruefully acknowledged that 'discrepancies may be detected in the details, errors in chronology, errors in geography, and errors in the orthography of names and the designation of persons' – that is, Cadwaladr was unable to remember when and where some events had happened, and who had been involved.[45] While Williams could assure readers that she had checked the information she received where possible (and had discovered that some of it contained major 'exaggerations'), she was unable to assure them that much of Cadwaladr's story was factually accurate. In her Preface she likens her task in writing the *Autobiography* to recreating a ruined tapestry:

> To seize the floating end of each subject that chanced to present itself, to draw it out, to disentangle it, to piece it, to set the warp straight and firmly in the loom, and to cast the woof aright, so as to produce the true and original pattern of such tapestry, has required sedulous application. The winding of silkworms' cocoons without a reel is scarcely a task of more difficult manipulation.[46]

The point of this extended metaphor is that the original tapestry no longer existed; in its place was a jumble of threads. In her attempt to recreate it Williams had had to take hold of the end of each loose thread in turn, carefully disentangle it, work out which other thread it needed to be joined to and spin ('piece') them together and then fix them to the loom and start the process of reweaving. It implies that in writing the *Autobiography* Williams wove a tapestry which used the same threads as the original and probably bore some resemblance to it, but was essentially her own creation; the previous tapestry had left no clear markers or outlines of its design which she could use as the basis for the new one. The comparison in her second sentence also implies the lack of a stable and clearly defined point around which the new work could be fitted; the raw material might be capable of being spun into silk, but without a firm basis it could very easily become a mere confused heap.

The passage of time and the destruction of records mean that it is impossible now to check much of the factual information in the *Autobiography*, but on some points its account of Cadwaladr's life is demonstrably inaccurate; research into the records of the ships she sailed on has shown that they did not visit many of the countries and ports she claimed to have visited and that she could not have been at the scene of some of the exciting events she describes. While it is possible (if one is charitable) to attribute these errors to a confusion between ships and voyages in her memory many years later, there is no such excuse for her account of the drowning of her first fiancé and her dramatic reaction to it: the research shows conclusively that his ship was wrecked off Milford Haven, not Liverpool, and – crucially – that all the crew were saved.[47] The version in the *Autobiography*, however, makes a far better story than the truth.

The same thing is true of the *Autobiography*'s account of her age. She was ten years old, not five, when her mother died, and this both affects her age at the time of later events and makes her childhood determination and self-reliance less impressive than the *Autobiography* suggests.[48] Although she prefaces the reference to her age at the time of the interviews for the book with several caveats, the *Autobiography* finally records her as saying, 'I believe I am now about sixty-one years of age' when (since records show she had been born in 1789) she was sixty-six or sixty-seven, depending on whether she said this before or after her birthday in May (1856).[49] The reason for this lie becomes clear when one turns to Nightingale's Nurses Register, in which Cadwaladr's age was recorded in autumn 1854 as fifty-four (this would have meant she had been born in 1800, making the arithmetic easier when asked her age later).[50] If Cadwaladr had told Williams her correct age, friends and supporters of Nightingale, who would certainly read the book, would know that she had lied about her age on recruitment as a nurse and would have used this to discredit the book's criticisms of Nightingale;[51] if she had given Williams an age consistent with the one she had given the Nurses' Register the discrepancy between that and her true age (eleven years) would have been great enough to attract the attention of people who had known her when she was growing up in Bala or working in Liverpool. The age Cadwaladr gave Williams neatly bisected the difference between her true age and the age she had given the Nurses' Register; with luck it was not far enough from either to attract the hostile attention of Nightingale's supporters or Cadwaladr's old acquaintances. The range and number of these inaccuracies act as a reminder that an autobiography presents its subject's life as the subject would prefer to remember it (or prefer readers to see it), and Cadwaladr's is no exception.

The fact that Cadwaladr's life is mediated through Jane Williams, however, means that Cadwaladr chose the way she presented herself to Williams, and Williams then chose from this what she wanted to present to the reader. The *Autobiography* constantly describes Cadwaladr as efficient both at managing her own life and looking after others, but many incidents show her as rash, gullible and self-centred. If Cadwaladr had written the book herself, then this contrast would have revealed her lack of self-awareness; the fact that Williams chose to include these incidents suggests that readers are being invited to see Cadwaladr as Williams saw her, not as she saw herself.

Certainly Williams makes her presence very obvious throughout the book. The narrative of Cadwaladr's life is preceded by William's Preface and Introduction, and followed by a Note, three Appendices and a Postscript; taken together, this material occupies a quarter of the book's pages. Further, each chapter is headed by an epigraph (from Shakespeare, Spenser, Milton, Pope, Cowper, Bacon, Thomas Campbell, Francis Quarles, James Montgomery and others), indicating a depth and breadth of knowledge of English literature which nothing in Cadwaladr's life or comments suggests she possessed. A further feature of the book which makes the reader aware of Williams's role in the composition of the book is the presence of her footnotes.

Some of these are conventional enough, giving more detail or background information on aspects of Cadwaladr's life; others, however, have a very different function. Some correct information in the narrative, indicating, for example, that a reference to 'Argyle' Castle (which does not exist) should be 'Inverary' (which is in Argyll).[52] Another footnote communicates an amused disbelief in a 'strange monster' which Cadwaladr declared she saw in the West Indies; it had a head like a shark, holes for ears, six wings, twelve feet and was green with a belly the colour of oyster shells, its front part 'feathery' and its hindquarters 'shelly'. Williams's reaction to this barrage of improbable details comes in a footnote which consists entirely of a sardonic verse by Cowper:

> 'Can this be true?' an arch observer cries,
> 'Yes' (rather moved) 'I saw it with these eyes.'
> 'Sir, I believe you, on that ground alone;
> I could not, had I seen it with my own.'[53]

Footnotes like these, which draw attention to an inaccuracy in the narrative or demonstrate deep scepticism about information the narrative presents as true, make it clear that Cadwaladr decided what went into the narrative and that Williams had control of the footnotes. This is shown particularly clearly where the expected footnote is missing. The narrative states as a fact that the father of Cadwaladr's persistent Portuguese suitor, Barbosa, 'was brother to King John the Eighth of Portugal'. The dates of other historical figures mentioned in the narrative are given in footnotes, and Williams's later footnotes on members of the Portuguese royal family show that she had read its history, but there is no footnote for 'King John the Eighth'.[54] The reason is that he did not exist; the last 'King John' (Joaõ) of Portugal, who from his dates is most likely to be the king in question, was the sixth - and the fact that 'the Eighth' is written in words rather than Roman numerals removes the possibility of a proof-reader's mistake. It seems that Cadwaladr's memory told her that Barbosa had said 'the Eighth' and that she refused to accept the historical evidence that either he or she was wrong.

One of the elements of the *Autobiography* which communicates the strongest sense of Cadwaladr's personality is the language in which her adventures, and her reactions to them, are described. This is the feature which has convinced many readers that the narrative of her life is an early work of oral history and that Williams took down Cadwaladr's words and (possibly correcting grammar and vocabulary and cutting out repetitions, etc.) used her account verbatim.[55] Certainly there are major differences in sentence structure and vocabulary between the narrative and the sections of the book where Williams was writing in her own (literary) persona; typically the language of the narrative is much simpler in structure, and uses everyday vocabulary, in contrast to the greater structural complexity and more formal vocabulary of the other sections.

The difference in reactions to news of the British army's involvement in the Crimean War is a case in point. The narrative describes how Cadwaladr heard the news and responded to it:

> After having been abroad, I always liked to know what was going on in the world, and this curiosity made me an eager reader of the newspapers. Sitting one evening with my sister, I read in one of them an account of the Battle of the Alma.
>
> 'Oh!', said I, 'if I had wings, would I not go!'
>
> 'What', answered Bridget, 'go to be a soldier? Well, I can believe anything, if you have changed your mind about them.'[56]

Williams's account of popular reaction to the same news (in Appendix B) uses a very different style:

> The long preceding peace of Europe, the unbroken practice of industrious arts and quiet labours, the existence of a majority among the population

> to whom war was known only as an old tradition or a distant rumour, caused surprise to mingle with compassion at the first information [of the Battle of the Alma] which reached Britain of the occurrence of the sufferings inalienably incident to warlike operations.[57]

The first passage shows Cadwaladr telling her affectionately sceptical sister of her decision to go to the Crimea in vivid and colloquial language ('Oh!', 'What', 'Well', 'said I'), and short sentences with a simple structure. The second is written in the style of a sociologist analysing the public reaction to the news of the battle in one long sentence which uses Latin-derived vocabulary ('majority of the population', 'occurrence', 'inalienably incident', 'operations') and abstract nouns ('peace', 'tradition' 'surprise', 'information', 'sufferings', 'operations'); it takes the reader very far from the lived experience of soldiers in filthy, blood-stained uniforms with untreated, maggot-infested wounds. In contrast to the entirely personal reactions in the first passage, the second presents an analysis which distances the writer, and therefore the reader, from the people who reacted. Both styles are entirely appropriate in their contexts and both successfully achieve their very different purposes; together they illustrate the range of styles which Williams was able to deploy.

The Preface makes it very clear that in the same way that Cadwaladr's faulty memory meant that Williams had to recreate the tapestry of events of Cadwaladr's life, so she had to use her skill and judgment to recreate on the page the characteristics of Cadwaladr's speaking voice. In her Preface, Williams explains that:

> It was impossible in all parts to give the exact language spoken. The writer has therefore aimed at conveying a true reflex of her exact meaning, preferring the general sense to literary [i.e. literal] precision. Wherever the very words of the heroine were apt and striking, they were retained.[58]

Williams's use of the word 'reflex' – in context, 'reflection' – indicates that she saw the narrative of the *Autobiography* as presenting Cadwaladr's 'meaning' at an angle of refraction rather than directly. She does not explain why using some of Cadwaladr's 'exact language spoken' was 'impossible', although the judgement as to which of Cadwaladr's 'words' were sufficiently 'apt and striking' to be used was clearly hers. The result is that while some of the language of the narrative is genuinely Cadwaladr's, some of it is Williams's pastiche of Cadwaladr's speaking style – and it is impossible to know which is which. The narrative is a work of ventriloquism, moving seamlessly between Cadwaladr's own words and style and William's imitation of them. As with much else in the *Autobiography*, below a surface of apparent simplicity many more complicated – and very interesting – things are going on.

Taken together, these three examples of life writing show that, while Williams embarked on them because of Hall's prompting, she immersed herself in the possibilities of the genre: she found out what she could do with it and what it could give to her as a writer, and then, having gained from the experience, she moved on. Her next published work took her into an entirely new genre, very much of her own choosing; and this, too, brought new and different possibilities.

4

Decisions and Directions

The book in which Jane Williams had invested so many hopes was finally published in 1861: *The Literary Women of England, including a Biographical Epitome of all the most Eminent to the Year 1700, and Sketches of the Poetesses to the Year 1850; with Extracts from their Works, and Critical Remarks.* As its title indicates, the book's focus is on poets rather than prose writers; Williams held the traditional view that poetry carried a higher status than prose, declaring: 'Verse constitutes the earliest literature of all nations, and through all ages it embodies the highest.'[1] Because she excludes prose writers after 1700 she says nothing about writers on female education and social rights such as Mary Wollstonecraft and Mary Astell or novelists such as Fanny Burney, Maria Edgeworth, Jane Austen and the Brontë sisters; and where an author wrote in other genres also, the non-poetry is given very little attention.

The epigraph to the Introduction, an extract from Craik's *Pursuit of Knowledge Under Difficulties: Female Examples*, makes explicit the book's theme: women have distinguished themselves in a wide range of intellectual activities 'against all sorts of disadvantages and discouragements, in the face of opinion and prejudice, in despite of means and facilities on the whole very inferior to those which the other sex has enjoyed', but their achievements have been under-valued or ignored.[2] Williams's Introduction to *The Literary Women of England* expressed the hope that the book would inspire girls not only to read and study literature by giving them examples of women in previous ages who had done this successfully, but that these examples would demonstrate that they themselves could become writers. The book's very existence proved that a woman could become a published author, and to emphasise this Williams gave her readers a personal anecdote:

> The simple name of a nursery-book, 'Aunt Mary's Tales for her Nieces', or some other has, 'ere now, taught a thoughtful child to infer – Then a woman could write and publish what she has seen and known; and why should not I, when I grow up, do the like?[3]

The point needed to be made explicitly, since the degree of prejudice which a woman author faced could be formidable. A review of *The Literary Women of England* in *The Examiner*, an influential and widely-read London-based journal, opens with the following paragraph:

> Literature is not the best business for a woman . . . [Women] have been wisest when they are content to have used their skills in other and more fitting ways. So it has been from the beginning . . . Large-hearted women can confer the greatest benefit upon their age when they are content unobtrusively to help others instead of seeking literary reputation for themselves. [Most] studious women have wisely preferred to exercise their influence quietly in the training up of their children, and in the cultivation of refined thoughts within their own friendly circle.[4]

The reviewer's verdict was clear before the book itself was even mentioned; by writing and – even worse – publishing their work, both the book's author and the women writers it discussed showed their lack of wisdom and propriety in failing to understand their correct – 'unobtrusive' and 'quiet' – place in the 'natural' intellectual, moral and social order.

Another reviewer (in the *Morning Post*), while taking a self-consciously more liberal stance ('Literature is a common ground between men and women') made it clear that male and female writers each had 'their proper sphere' ordained by 'Nature', and should stay there. In literature, the review declared, 'the severe and laborious departments are more particularly the province of the stronger [sex], while the more delicate disports by choice in the livelier realms of fancy and the gay bowers of love'. Fortunately, English women knew their place and 'with a ready perception of the right have adapted themselves instinctively to the path assigned to them'.[5] For a woman to write on subjects in 'the severe and laborious departments' was therefore against both 'Nature' and what was 'proper'; according to this reviewer, the subjects on which Jane Williams wrote made her an anomaly who 'disport[ed]' herself in entirely the wrong genres.

There is only one point in Williams's writings when she explicitly confronted women's place in the society she lived in; perhaps writing a book which inevitably included examples of the constraints on women's education and autonomy through the centuries made her aware that she needed to warn her young readers of the realities they faced. Her Introduction to *The Literary Women of England* includes this description of the contrast between the public sphere of men's lived experience and the private sphere to which Victorian society aimed to confine women:

> Men stand, as it were, upon a promontory, commanding extensive views, and open to immediate impulses from all above, below and around them. Women sit like genii of secluded caves, receiving echoes and communicating mere reverberations from the outer world, but not without their own pure springs and rills, tinkling with music and fraught with peculiar efficacy.[6]

Her points are made through a series of binary opposites. Men's place is high up in the open air, from which they have a panoramic view over the landscape below them; women are confined to an enclosed space below ground level. Men are able to see clearly the world around them and engage actively with it; women's restricted line of sight means that the information they receive is at best limited and at worst distorted (the image suggests Plato's metaphor of men in a cave who mistake shadows for reality because of their limited range of vision). Men stand up and are active, open to 'immediate impulses'; women sit passively 'receiving echoes' and therefore can obtain only second-hand information which they cannot communicate effectively to others. The assertion in the second sentence that women have their own pure sources which carry women-specific values ('fraught with peculiar efficacy') is presented as a very limited consolation for female disadvantage; 'not without' implies major limitations. And while the reference to 'genii of secluded caves' near 'pure springs and soft rills' recalls the female oracles of Classical antiquity, the women merely *voiced* those oracles; the inspiration for their messages came from the (male) god.[7] There is an (almost certainly conscious) irony in the way Williams here uses allusions to Classical literature and history – regarded at the time as almost exclusively the intellectual province of men – to illustrate the limitations which the society she lived in imposed on women's educational, intellectual and social experience; in the same way that the book – by a woman author and about women authors – demonstrated to the girls it was written for that writing literature was not a male-only prerogative, so her choice of images showed that women could have access to the 'serious and laborious' fields of learning which the *Morning Post* reviewer regarded as intended by 'Nature' for men only. Williams's book offered the 'lives, principles and sentiments' of women writers as exemplars to her youthful readers, but it also presented them with a grimly realistic view of their (in many ways, marginal) position in Victorian society.

The Literary Women of England covers more than a thousand years and summarises the lives and writings of more than a hundred women. As well as their works and biographies of them (where these existed), her book also draws on seventeen histories of women's writing and related reference books; Classical Greek and Latin authors, Dante, Machiavelli and the Anglo-Saxon Chronicle, all in translation; histories of Britain, medieval Europe, the Christian Church and the Jewish people; the Welsh Triads, histories, medieval law and the Iolo manuscripts; books on botany, geology and zoology; books on English language and literary theory, and the major (male) English poets from Spenser to Southey; writing on French literary theory, and the works of Madame de Staël (both in the original). *The Literary Women of England* represents a massive amount of research as well as writing, and it is not surprising that it took many years' work to produce and see through the press.

This extensive reading is used to establish an impressive intellectual context for the entries on individual female writers; many of Williams's comments are sharp and perceptive, and the breadth of her selection of authors, and the examples of their work, would undoubtedly have introduced many readers to authors previously unknown to them. Unfortunately for her hopes for the book's success, however, its whole is considerably less than the sum of its parts.

There are two main reasons for this; one lies in the disproportionate attention given to one writer. In her Introduction Williams explains that she had planned to write 'a Critical and Biographical Essay' on the life and poetry of Felicia Hemans, but that she 'was induced to enlarge [her] plan'. The book's contents suggest she was unwilling to waste any of the material she had collected; approximately one-fifth is devoted to Hemans's life and work. Further, Williams explains that 'in order to leave with the reader a favourable impression of the Literary Women of England' she decided that the book should end with Hemans's 166-line poem 'Despondency and Aspiration' – a decision which implies that the poem represented the most dazzling example of female literary achievement during the previous thousand years. The consequence is that the book's view of the Literary Women's writing is very partial – in both senses.[8]

The second reason for the book's overall failure lies in Williams's attempts to please two different readerships with conflicting interests and priorities. The first was the girls for whom the book was written; the second was their parents, guardians and teachers – the adult gatekeepers who would decide which books were acceptable for the girls to read. Many of the authors featured in *The Literary Women of England* had succeeded in becoming writers and scholars in the face of opposition and obstruction – often created by *their* adult gatekeepers. This was a period when a book by a woman on the education of girls could castigate a 'strong-minded girl' as 'dogmatic and presumptuous, self-willed and arrogant, eccentric in dress and disagreeable in manner', and warn that the line between 'a learned woman' and a 'strong-minded female' was dangerously thin;[9] by showing girls that it was not only possible but admirable for them to become writers and scholars, Williams was encouraging them to challenge the assumptions of society in general and their adult gatekeepers in particular.

Many of the 'literary women' featured in her book had done exactly that, and – even worse in the eyes of their gatekeepers – had done it successfully. Laetitia Barbauld's father 'cherished the ordinary prejudice against learned women', but finally yielded to 'her urgent entreaties' and acknowledged 'her masculine capacity for study'; Hannah More's father was also initially 'alarmed . . . lest she should become that dreaded monster, a learned woman', but was eventually persuaded by 'his less prejudiced wife' to allow their daughter to continue studying; Anna Seward's father at first refused to allow her to read literature, insisting that instead she spent her time in 'strictly feminine accomplishments . . . especially ornamental needlework' but withdrew his veto after his daughter agreed to give up her 'first love'.[10] Williams's choice of vocabulary invites her readers to mock the 'prejudiced' fathers who regarded an educated woman as either an honorary man or a 'dreaded monster' and, while it warned that the emotional cost could be high (certainly in Seward's case), assured them that if they persisted they would eventually be permitted to escape the boredom of a life devoted to 'ornamental needlework'. However, examples of parental authority being mocked, challenged and circumvented were hardly likely to recommend the book to the gatekeepers; while Williams encouraged the girls to emulate the intellectual and literary achievements of 'the cleverest of women' (Madame de Staël, whom she quoted extensively), the gatekeepers were more likely to favour Charles Kingsley's poetic advice: that the way 'to earn yourself a purer poet's laurel / Than Shakespeare's crown' was to 'Be good, sweet maid, and let who will, be clever'.[11] Williams had to reassure the gatekeepers that literary women could be both.

She accordingly declared that no 'intellectual pursuit' could justify 'the neglect of even the smallest act of domestic duty'. If an unmarried woman writer had no parents or unmarried male relatives who needed her 'domestic duty' she should serve the community in which she lived; Jane Taylor, for example, 'gave herself up . . . to nurse the sick, to teach poor children and to make herself useful among her friends . . . pursuing meanwhile her literary occupations whenever health and leisure allowed'.[12] (Jane Taylor herself declared that a woman could take pleasure in both 'making a fine pudding' and 'reading a fine poem', although possibly not simultaneously).[13] The goal, however, was marriage, and at the end of her survey of female authors before 1700, Williams declared triumphantly: 'the greater number of these literary Englishwomen were married, and many of them more than once, from which it would appear that their mental pursuits had not weakened their domestic affections.'[14] She had to reassure her readers that it was possible for a woman to be simultaneously married *and* literary.

Hemans presented an excellent example. After her husband left, she needed to support herself and her five sons and pay for their education, so that writing for money could be seen as an extension of her maternal role – the very definition of femininity – rather than as personal ambition for fame or fortune. Further, her poetry celebrated the virtues of hearth and home, describing 'domestic bliss' where the angel of the hearth was in command: 'Her empire, home! her throne, affection's breast!' One of her early volumes even bore the reassuring title *The Domestic Affections*.[15]

Williams's attempt to show the gatekeepers that her other literary women were equally aware of their domestic and moral duties ran into problems when she discussed writers of a period when these duties were deeply unfashionable: the later seventeenth and early eighteenth centuries. Some minor writers of this period could be safely mentioned (they used 'their moderate abilities for the promotion of good morals and piety') while others, notably Susannah Centlivre and Delarivier Manley, were rebuked for allowing their 'cleverness and wit' to be corrupted by the 'indelicacy' of the era.[16] Aphra Behn, however, was another matter.

Williams's attitude to Behn changes throughout the entry on her, first describing her as leading 'a gay, perhaps licentious life' (both 'gay' and 'perhaps licentious' suggest an amused tolerance), then moving from 'the licentious indelicacy of [Behn's] lively writings' (a more negative description, tempered by the positive connotations of 'lively') to the unequivocal statement that Behn 'is the first English authoress upon record whose life was openly wrong and whose writings were obscene' and apologising for mentioning her at all: 'Her name would have been excluded from all mention in these pages had it not been necessary to mark the true state of female literature at this period.'[17] Williams was clearly aware that to parents and teachers Behn was an irredeemably notorious figure and that, in order to reassure these gatekeepers that her own book was morally sound, it would be better to condemn too much than not enough.

Williams's censorious view of Restoration authors in general and Behn in particular makes interesting reading when set beside a poem she composed in 1851 while staying at Llanover Court.[18] Lord Torrington, another of the guests, said that he had heard she wrote occasional verse, occasionally, and 'entreated [her] to write his character in verse'; she produced a poem the following day for the assembled company (first showing it to the Halls for their approval). Lord Torrington had a reputation as a rake and libertine, and Williams's initial response when she heard he would be joining the house party had been one of prim disapproval ('unwise were they who sent him to govern Ceylon!'). After she met him, however, she came to see him differently, and over the following days she described him in her diary (copied in a letter to her aunt) as 'very chatty and agreeable', 'full of fun and lively anecdotes' and 'irresistibly droll' ('irresistibly' is particularly revealing). She was clearly flattered that he continually sought her company, reporting that Augusta Hall 'says that I shall be [his] head favourite before he goes' (which comes close to an uncharacteristic simper). The verse she produced in response to his request was brief and pointed:

> Perchance this pencil might not greatly err
> Should it compare thee to a Rochester;
> Thy social grace, wit, pleasantry and whim
> In gay profanity resemble him:
> May favouring Time the parallel pursue
> And send, some happy day, thy Burnet too!

While many of Rochester's verses were regarded at this period as too obscene for publication, Williams's poem shows that she was familiar not only with his reputation but with the facts of his life; her letter explicitly refers to Bishop Burnet as 'the means of converting Lord Rochester'. Her attitude to both Rochester and Torrington is made clear in the third and fourth lines of the poem, in which only 'profanity' carries negative implications; as her other diary entries reveal, she – entirely unconsciously – found him very attractive. She had the satisfaction of knowing that her poem hit home: when she read it aloud he turned very pale, and later responded with a poem which, while demonstrating an aristocratic disregard for rhyme, metre and syntax, praised her as 'All that is gentle, soft and kind, / A Rock of Virtue' and begged her, when in heaven singing psalms with King David, to remember her 'Rochester'. Another member of the house party was the Irish writer Sydney Owenson, Lady Morgan, whose role seems to have been that of licensed court jester (while other guests' party pieces included composing impromptu riddles and playing Classical piano music, Lady Morgan entertained the assembled company with the – literal – gallows humour of the Irish comic song 'The Night before Larry was Stretched'). She seems to have enjoyed drawing attention to subjects which everyone else was carefully avoiding and then watching their reactions; at this point she joined in, with a poem which compared Williams to a Saint who was also 'a Charmer' and Torrington to a 'Gay' Demon, and declared that their poetic skirmish

> Left it little in doubt that with each, each was charmed,
> Or who in the end would turn up the winner:
> The Demon turn Saint or the Saint turn [a] Sinner.

An amused and relaxed attitude to a poet generally regarded as one of the most 'licentious' and 'obscene' in English literature was clearly entirely acceptable within the sophisticated literary and social circle at Llanover; it was emphatically not appropriate in a book directed at impressionable young girls whose parents had to be assured that it would protect, rather than endanger, their moral welfare.

Both *The Literary Women of England*'s disproportionate attention to Hemans and the unresolved tension inherent in its attempt to persuade each of two opposing groups that it was on their side, suggest that Williams did not give herself enough distance from her material to achieve the perspective that would have enabled her to revise a draft into a well-balanced book. This may have been influenced by a wish that it should be published as soon as possible after the delays caused by her work on *The Autobiography of Elizabeth Davis* which, as her Preface to it shows, had taken far longer than she had expected. And there are other indications of haste, including a significant lack of clarity over terms used in the book's title.

At different points in the book *Literary* has to be understood as 'writing literature' or as 'having literary interests' or as 'acting as patron to authors' or 'being literate' (two woman are included because they were able to write their names[19]). *England* also has a remarkably wide reach, apparently including not only Ireland, Scotland and Wales but also Italy and medieval Germany[20]. 'English' and 'British' are used interchangeably – certainly a common practice at the time, but very surprising from Williams.[21] And in an age when 'British' often meant 'Welsh' – and when Williams used it in this sense at one point in *The Literary Women* ('the Ancient British Bards [who composed the Triads]') – it is astonishing to see that she, the author of *Artegall, Cambrian Tales*, the biography of Carnhuanawc and the autobiography of Betsi Cadwaladr, could not only write that 'the British Empire [covers] all the regions ruled by the British tongue' but could leave the statement unrevised for publication[22].

It is probably wise, therefore, to see *The Literary Women of England* as a collection of interesting and often lively comments and literary judgements rather than as a history of women's writing in English; certainly many of her comments and judgements are perceptive, entertaining or both. Lady Pembroke's elegy on her brother, Sir Phillip Sidney, had 'delicacy and elegance, both of thought and expression', for example, while Anna Seward's biography of Erasmus Darwin was 'not merely inelegant, pedantic and replete with affectation, it is absolutely and daringly ungrammatical.

Most of the words are English, but the structure of the sentences belong[s] to no language living or dead.'[23] Other judgements damn with faint praise: a poem by Laetitia Barbauld 'is good as far as it goes'.[24] Overall, though, there is a gusto in her destructive criticism which her praise lacks. Even the much-admired Hemans can be convicted of bad writing; her *Sebastian of Portugal* 'comes to an untimely end, dying out from mere inanity'.[25]

At the level of detail, *The Literary Women of England* is sharp and clear. Its weaknesses lie in the constantly shifting uses of key terms, the disproportionate amount of space given to Hemans and its contradictory messages to two very different readerships: its attempt to assure parents that girls could pursue scholarly and literary ambitions and still be dutiful daughters, while telling girls that they might have to stop being dutiful daughters in order to pursue their scholarly and literary ambitions. Whatever the reasons for Williams's uncharacteristic lack of precision and clarity, the outcome is that the book did not fulfil her hopes for it. It did not mark the beginning of a new direction in her writing, or establish her name with a new, wider, readership, or lead to enough interest in the writers it featured to justify her producing new editions of their work. Instead, years of research and writing had led to very little. Some writers in this situation would have analysed the reasons for the failure, chosen another subject likely to appeal to a wide readership, and tried again. Williams's response was very different.

The following year she published a book whose title showed that she was abandoning her attempt to reach a wider, Anglocentric readership: *Celtic Fables, Fairy Tales and Legends, chiefly from Ancient Welsh Originals*. Her books published in the twelve years before *The Literary Women of England* (*Artegall*, *Cambrian Tales*, her biography of Carnhuanawc and the autobiography of Betsi Cadwaladr) had all used her personal knowledge of, and contact with, living Welsh people. After the failure of *The Literary Women of England* to achieve hoped-for success she turned again to Welsh subjects, but her later writing focused on people and events from the distant Welsh past and relied on documentary sources; the picture it presented of Wales and Welsh culture was essentially antiquarian.

Certainly the mid-nineteenth century saw a fashion in Britain for a re-imagined medieval world – especially one with a Celtic flavour – in different art forms. In literature there was Dinah Craik's *Avillion and Other Tales* (1854), William Morris's *The Defence of Guinevere and Other Poems* (1858) and Tennyson's *Idylls of the King* (begun in 1856, published in 1859); in painting, Dante Gabriel Rossetti's frescoes for the Oxford Union in 1858 which included scenes from stories of Arthur, Merlin, Sir Gawain and La Belle Iseult. Matthew Arnold's lectures on Celtic literature (given in 1865, published in 1867) reflect a similar appropriation of medieval Celtic culture by an Englishman for his own purposes.

As well as these re-imaginings and imitations, this interest in the medieval past also expressed itself by making genuine early or medieval literature available in translation to a wider reading public: Ab Ithel's *Y Gododdin* (1852), Thomas Wright's edition of Malory's *Morte d'Arthur* (1858) and – especially relevant in this context – the translation of the *Mabinogion* (published in one volume in 1848) by Lady Charlotte Guest, another member of the Llanover circle. The popularity of these translations and reworkings of texts from the Celtic past may have suggested to Williams that it would be an opportune moment to publish the poems on Celtic legends and fairy tales she had written over the previous thirty years, which she had 'versified' (her word from the book's title page) in English; but the tone of most of her versions was very different from that of the solemn and often sentimental treatment of Celtic legends by other writers.

Celtic Fables contains ten poems: nine narrate a legend or story and the tenth, which is much shorter, acts as a pendant to one of the longer poems. Nine of the poems are based on Welsh sources, the tenth on a Cornish folk story. Of the nine poems with Welsh sources, seven are based on fables in the Iolo Morganwg manuscripts, held in the Llanover library after the Halls bought them from Iolo's son Taliesin Williams in 1848; they had been published with English translations in the same year.[26] The origins of Iolo's fables have been tactfully described as 'a major puzzle', since it is impossible to know how much is his invention, how much is his 'manipulation of tradition' and how much 'represents his sources more or less faithfully'[27] – a particularly relevant caveat, since Iolo's fables include Aesop's 'The Ant and the Grasshopper', which had been well known in English translation for centuries (and which Williams used for her collection). The remaining two poems (the first 'Legend of Llynsafaddan' and 'Elidwr') are based on anecdotes in the twelfth-century *Itinerarium Kambriae* (The Journey through Wales) by Giraldus Cambrensis translated by Sir Richard Colt Hoare (published in 1806). Three of Williams's poems (the two 'Legends of Llynsafaddan' and the Cornish 'Funeral among the Small People') had been included in *Cambrian Tales*, where they were presented as compositions by sympathetic characters.

In *Cambrian Tales* Williams had shown herself a sensitive and knowledgeable observer of the natural world in Wales, with detailed descriptions of landscapes, flora and fauna. Fables are traditionally set everywhere and nowhere, but four of the poems based on fables in *Celtic Fables* are explicitly set in the part of Wales she knew best – 'The Mole and the Lark' near the Black Mountains and 'The Two Fishes' on the banks of the Wye – while 'The Grasshopper and the Ant' is set among 'Cambrian scenes'; and although the setting of 'The Wood Pigeon and the Magpie' is not named, it has the characteristics of the Welsh countryside in spring. Her other poems from Welsh sources have explicitly Welsh settings: the two 'Legends of Llynsafaddan' are set around the eponymous lake, 'Elidwr' takes place on the banks of the Towy, while 'The Ancients of the World' travels from Scotland to Gwent, north-west Wales, the Wirral and Ceredigion.

The three shorter 'fable' poems follow their originals both in their plots and morals. In 'The Mole and the Lark' and 'The Two Fishes', the Mole who envies the Lark her freedom in the air (lamenting his lot 'to dwell and grovel in the dark / A groping Mole and not a joyous Lark!') and the Fish who ambitiously leaps on to the river bank and then realises he is stranded ('Rash, self-deluding creature!'[28]) both come to understand that they should have stayed in their own element. The moral of 'The Wood Pigeon and the Magpie' is that advice and education are wasted on those who refuse to recognise that they need them ('Of self-conceit and false pretence / Comes ignorance of ignorance').[29] The moral lesson is that the status quo must be accepted, and that any attempt to break the mould – or help others to do so – is doomed.

Other poems vary Williams's originals in interesting ways – for example, by stopping before the end. The first 'Legend of Llynsafaddan' is the only poem in the collection which follows its source both in naming its characters (the Welsh Prince Gruffydd and the Normans Earl Milo and Payn-Fitz-John) and in setting it in a specific historical period (the reign of Henry I). One winter's day Gruffydd is riding past Llynsafaddan in the company of the two Norman lords, one of whom tauntingly mentions the Welsh legend that the birds on the lake will sing only on the command of the rightful ruler. Gruffydd suggests that since the Normans rule Wales, the two lords should test the legend; they both try, and fail. They then insist that Gruffydd tries; he prays to 'his father's God' before asking the birds to proclaim him the rightful ruler – at which they burst into full-throated song. The poem does not explain whether they needed divine help to recognise the true ruler – and, given the way legends operate, it is not surprising that the birds ignore the Normans' arrogant commands and obey the respectful Gruffydd. In Williams's source the Norman lords report the incident to Henry I, who replies that it is 'not a matter of so much wonder: for although by our great authority we commit acts of violence and wrong against these people, yet they are known to be the rightful inheritors of this land'.[30] The king recognises the moral right of Gruffydd's claim while making it clear that this will have no effect on his decision; the Normans will continue to rule Wales, no matter how enthusiastically the birds sing.

Williams's version of 'A Funeral among the Small People' also omits her source's ending. Richard is returning from St Ives with a load of pilchards when he sees lights inside Lelant church, goes to look through the window, and finds himself watching the touching and beautiful funeral of the Fairy Queen. The grief of the fairy mourners affects him so powerfully that he cries out in sympathy with them, and thus reveals his presence. Williams stops the action of her story at this moment; in her source the narrative continues, and Richard is punished for eavesdropping: 'Many [of the fairies] brushed past the terrified man and, shrieking, pierced him with sharp instruments. He was compelled to save his life *by the most rapid flight*.'[31] By ending where they do, both her poems prevent the protagonist from having to face unwelcome truths: that having moral right on one's side is no protection against brute force, and that the world of fantasy and imagination can bring pain and disillusion as well as beauty and pleasure.

'Elidwr', the second poem in the collection based on an anecdote from Giraldus Cambrensis, also shows a protagonist breaking the rules – but here the consequences are painful. Elidwr plays truant from school to 'pass the summer hours' on the banks of the Towy; on his second night there 'two tiny men' in green appear and lead him to the underground realm of Fairy Land, which is too beautiful for words to describe and where all the inhabitants are happy and productive. After a time he is permitted to return to the upper world to see his mother, who insists he brings her a token from Fairy Land to prove that his stories about it are true. On his next visit he takes with him a flower which turns into a heavy ball of gold on contact with the air of the 'real' world; he is pursued by two of the fairies, who snatch it back in the moment before his mother can take it. When he returns to the river bank, the cave through which he had entered Fairy Land 'was gone, removed, or vanished as a dream', never to reappear; he has broken the rules of the magical world and is permanently exiled from it. In Williams's source, the loss remains a source of pain for the rest of Elidwr's life; he 'could never relate the particulars [of his experience] without suddenly bursting into tears'.[32] Williams's version, however, suggests that he sublimated his pain at the loss of Fairy Land by scholarship and religious faith:

> At last, the weary-hearted wanderer sought
> And prized the privilege of cultured thought;
> Hence Elidwr, the Truant boy, appears
> The Scholar and the Priest in after years.[33]

Williams does not give reasons for choosing particular fables and legends rather than others (*Celtic Fables* is the only one of her books not to have a Preface) but some would certainly have held great resonance for her. The parallels between her own life and Elidwr's are obvious: both, while of school age, had a happy and apparently settled life snatched away from them and later found consolation in study and religious faith. It is easy to see how his story might have sparked an imaginative and creative response in her.

In Colt Hoare's translation of Giraldus, the entrance to Fairy Land is 'under the hollow bank of a river'. The Welsh term for a ledge, rim or (in this context) an overhanging bank is *ysgafell*;[34] in her poem Williams changes this to a cave. The resonance for her of the entrance to an enchanted land of perfect happiness and prosperity which had been reached via an *ysgafell* and later lost forever could well have been too painful to contemplate. And, like Elidwr, she found some relief in study for the lifelong sense of loss and exclusion; revealingly, the lines quoted above suggest he was a scholar first and a priest second. Her poem, which draws on her abilities and experience both as a scholar and a poet, can be seen as performing the work of consolation it describes.

The second 'Legend of Llynsafaddan', which ends the collection, would also have had considerable personal resonance. It relates to her early life, to her knowledge of the area she was living in when she wrote it, and to her first publication. In a departure from her source, it includes a reference to the river Llynfi, a tributary of the Wye which it joins at Glasbury; in her poem 'Lines on the Banks of the Llunvey' (*sic*) in *Miscellaneous Poems* she had used the river as a metaphor for the rapid reverses of fortune which life can bring. If the Llynfi held some painful memories, it was also associated with a period in her life which had seen the publication of her first book and allowed her to find her own literary voice.

The source for her poem shows how punishment inevitably follows crime and that not only the guilty suffer. A noble lady who had refused to marry her poor suitor changes her mind when he becomes rich after murdering a travelling merchant; a 'sepulchral' voice promises reassuringly that retribution will be deferred for nine generations. When finally the penalty has to be paid, the murderer's descendants are drowned in a great flood which destroys the nearby town and its inhabitants. (Surprisingly, Williams omits her source's most vivid detail: that after the town is swallowed by the lake, three chimney tops, still emitting smoke, are visible above the water, and that on its surface floats a pair of gloves conveniently bearing the name and coat of arms of the murdered merchant.[35]) Her ending not only varies from her source in the Iolo manuscripts by implying that the town's disappearance was caused by an earthquake (the explanation of its destruction in an alternative version of the story[36]), but adds a completely new – and in context, surprising – consequence:

> Terrific rumblings rend the earth,
> Lo, vengeance, ruin and despair!
> And where the Murderer's turrets rose,
> The Lake is spread, and Llynfi flows.[37]

The last half-line, which introduces a new and entirely unexpected element, comes close to suggesting that all the dramatic events of the poem were part of a Grand Design to create the River Llynfi.

This makes her choice to end the book with this poem particularly important. In *Miscellaneous Poems*, her biography of Carnhuanawc and *The Literary Women of England* she had followed (apparently deliberately) the example of Giraldus Cambrensis in *Journey through Wales* by using each book's final sequence as an expression of thoughts and feelings that were particularly important to her; the creation of the Llynfi gains an additional significance by its position as the last clause of the last line of the last poem in the book.

The two remaining poems in the collection show Williams reworking her source material much more radically; here the differences from the originals are not merely a matter of new settings and details, of emphasising a particular aspect of her raw material or of omitting some elements, but of changing the focus of the stories so drastically that her poem's message is completely different from that of the original.

'The Ancients of the World" centres on a quest to find the oldest creature in existence; each one consulted by the protagonist refers him to another who is even older. This was a well-known trope in medieval Celtic legends, most notably in 'Culhwch and Olwen', one of the stories of the *Mabinogion*. In 'Culhwch and Olwen', however, it is part of one strand in a much more complex narrative; in 'The Ancients of the World', by contrast, the quest for the oldest creature provides the poem's storyline.

A Scottish Eagle's mate has died and he is looking for a replacement; from what he hears of the Owl of Cwmcawlwyd she seems suitable. He is a king Eagle, however, and owls have very low social status; to have offspring with such a plebeian bird would insult his royal lineage. Before he informs her that she is the chosen one, therefore, he wants to make sure that she is, in the words of Williams's source, 'past the age of child-bearing'.[38] To reassure himself about the Owl's advanced age, he goes first to the Stag of Rhedynvre, who refers him to the Salmon of Llyn Llivon, who refers him to the Ouzel of Cilgwri, who refers him to the Toad of Cors Fochno. (The Eagle lives in Scotland; although the Ancient Creatures live in different parts of Wales and north-west England, they are all members of the same community, which suggests that the original legend emerged from the period when parts of Scotland, northern England and Wales were ruled by the same dynasty – that is, before the early seventh century.) The Toad, indisputably the oldest of the Creatures, tells the Eagle that when he was a mere stripling the Owl was already a great-great-grandmother (and, says Williams's source, 'an old grey hag . . . frightening the children and disturbing everybody'[39]). This reassures the Eagle that their union will not (says the original alliteratively) bring 'on his tribe debasement or disgrace, degradation or degeneration' and that he can safely condescend to take her for his mate – and there Williams's source ends.[40]

Whereas the original fable is told 'straight', with the assumption that readers will naturally sympathise with the Eagle, Williams's version establishes an ironic distance between her readers and the characters, presenting the Ancient Creatures as if they were members of a Victorian gentlemen's club (for example, the Eagle regards the Stag as his 'antlered friend' and treats him as if he were a discreet family solicitor).[41]

The major difference in her retelling, however, is that she continues the story after the original ends. Whereas her source showed the (male) Creatures discussing the (female) Owl in detail, the Owl herself did not appear as a character in her own right and did not have a voice. In Williams's version the Owl appears, speaks, and has both opinions of her own and the confidence to express them. When the Eagle first met her he decided that:

> She was in truth the very bride he sought,
> So prudent, so discreet and so demure[42]

but when, having completed his inquiries, he returned to 'woo' her 'with confidence', neither she nor her response was what he expected; her eyes shone with a 'lurid light' and she 'rebuke[d]' him 'hoarsely' for consulting the Ancient Creatures before talking to her. She criticised his assumption that she would go to live with him in Scotland, and reminded him that 'the aged never like their home to change'; the older she was, the less likely she was to be willing to move.[43] She then gave him her definitive answer, in lines which end the poem:

> Sooner the Stag shall Rhedynvre forsake,
> Sooner the Salmon leave fair Llivon's lake,
> Sooner the Ouzel quit Cilgwri's thorn,
> Sooner the Toad desert Cors Fochno's bourn,
> Yea, sooner thou shalt shun thine ancient rock,
> Than I resign Cwmcawlwyd's sheltering nook;
> Return, proud Eagle, to thy lonely state,
> Cwmcawlwyd's Owl rejects thee for a mate.[44]

While the original version takes it for granted, in the conventional patriarchal way of traditional stories, that the Eagle's wishes are paramount and that the Owl will automatically acquiesce,

Williams's version makes the feminist assertion that the Owl has a mind of her own and is determined to live her life on her own terms. The ending that Williams gives the fable both exposes and subverts the masculinist assumptions of the original; it also exposes and subverts readers' expectations about traditional stories.

Legends, traditional stories and fairy tales all require a conclusion which involves change, in good ways for the heroes and bad for the villains: the Frog Prince and the Beast are turned back into handsome princes; Cinderella is saved from a life of drudgery, and marries Prince Charming; the Ogre and the Wicked Witch are killed. In Williams's version of this legend, however, no such change occurs; at the beginning of the story the Eagle is in Scotland looking for a mate and the Owl is living in Cwmcawlwyd on her own, and at the end of the story they are in exactly the same places and situations. Like her message to young readers in *The Literary Women of England*, the changes which Williams makes to her source for 'The Ancients of the World' assert that women have the right to make their own decisions in life; and if her poem carries a moral it is that fables and fairy tales do not always end as their protagonists – and readers – expect.

The other poem in *Celtic Fables* in which Williams changes completely the focus and message of the story is one which her readers would have known well, so that the differences between her version and the traditional one would have been conspicuous. 'The Ant and the Grasshopper' was one of Aesop's best-known fables, and had been familiar in English translations since the seventeenth century (even Iolo Morganwg could hardly have claimed that his version was original). One reason for its popularity was its simple, obvious moral: the thrifty, prudent Ant works hard through the summer so that he has enough food to last him through the winter, in contrast to the feckless, pleasure-loving Grasshopper who plays and sings the summer away and when winter comes begs the Ant – unsuccessfully – for food to keep him alive. Further, its moral chimed with familiar religious teaching, from the Old Testament's 'Go to the Ant, thou sluggard; consider her ways and be wise' to the New Testament parable of the wise and foolish virgins.[45] The traditional version of the fable led readers to empathise with the Ant – the protagonist – and to judge the Grasshopper by the Ant's criteria; the virtues and advantages of thrift, hard work and forward planning were so obvious that making the story's moral explicit was almost superfluous.

Williams's version changes her original in four ways. Firstly, the Grasshopper, not the Ant, is her protagonist (indicated by her change to the title: 'The Grasshopper and the Ant'), and events are recounted (although in the third person) from his perspective. The narrative establishes his sociability, good humour and the pleasure he gets and gives to his friends from his music, singing and dancing; he is 'blithe', 'full of mirth, galliard and song' and 'Had no thought of tomorrow, no wish but to please'.[46] The fact that the first half of the line echoes another biblical injunction ('Take no thought for the morrow'[47]) suggests that in this respect the Grasshopper is closer than the Ant to Christian teachings.

In Williams's original there is no suggestion that the Ant heard the Grasshopper's song while he was working during the summer, but in her version we are explicitly told that

> E'en the Ant, on grave errands of business bent,
> To provide for his family ever intent,
> Forgot anxious care, while in marching along,
> He heard the glad sound of the Grasshopper's song.[48]

The result is that when the Grasshopper asks for help, the Ant has not only the general moral obligation to help a fellow creature in distress, but a personal obligation to repay the Grasshopper for his song; his refusal to help is therefore even more culpable.

A third contrast between the two versions lies in their treatment of winter. In the original, winter arrives with depressing inevitability each year, so that preparing for it makes good sense; Williams's version treats winter as an extraordinary and unpredictable phenomenon, in which the effects of first frosts are compared to 'the sudden destruction of earthquake and fire'.[49] From this perspective, the Grasshopper's approach to life ('The present to him seemed a sort of forever'[50]) is entirely reasonable.

Her fourth major change lies in the brutal callousness of the Ant when the Grasshopper comes begging for food. While translators of Aesop had sometimes mitigated the Ant's refusal by explaining that giving food away would risk letting his family starve, one of the earliest English versions emphasised that 'Good Husbandry and Thrift' should not be used as a cover for avarice, and that 'the Necessities of our Neighbours have a Christian Right to what we have to spare'.[51] This makes the response of Williams's Ant particularly reprehensible; he treats the Grasshopper 'with contempt' instead of 'brotherly kindness', abuses him as an 'idler' and an 'improvident wretch', and turns him away contemptuously. Even when he sees the Grasshopper's corpse in front of his door the following morning, he feels no 'compunction'.[52] Williams gives him no redeeming qualities whatsoever.

The cumulative effect of these changes is that Williams's version resists any moral. The Ant is prudent and hardworking, but also smug, miserly and brutally callous; the Grasshopper is generous-spirited, happy and fulfilled as a creative artist whose work gives pleasure and enlarges the horizons of those who listen to him, but ends up dead – painfully. The moral of the traditional story has been completely subverted.

Although the poems in *Celtic Fables* show variety in their characters (fish, animals, birds, insects; named and unnamed human beings; creatures from another world) there are many similarities in their outcomes. None of the protagonists 'live happily ever after'; rather, they suffer failure and disappointment (the Eagle, the Magpie, Richard), loss (Elidwr) and even death (the Mole, the 'rash' Trout, the Grasshopper), while the creation of the river Llynfi causes the destruction of a community. Only the first 'Legend of Llynsafaddan' approaches a moment when the protagonist's wrongs are righted, and that moment is as fragile and transient as birdsong.

The *Celtic Fables* are set in a magic land in which birds, animals, fish and insects talk, and human beings are surrounded by supernatural beings and forces; but, as in fables and fairy stories, they reflect the real human world in their preoccupations and outcomes (an early definition of a fable is 'a fictitious story picturing a truth'[53]). As a genre, the fable has historically attracted writers outside the mainstream of the societies they lived in; the onlooker can often see events more clearly than those involved in them.[54] Williams was outside the mainstream as a writer; not only as a woman in a society that regarded a woman writer as an anomaly, but as a woman who wrote in 'severe and laborious' genres conventionally reserved for men. She was outside the mainstream of the Anglo-centric literary world in Britain; with the exception of *The Literary Women of England* her mature works drew on her knowledge of Wales, the Welsh language, literature, history and culture in her writing. She was also outside the mainstream in terms of social class; she had been born into a middle-class family, worked as a servant and now moved in the same social circles as aristocrats, diplomats, politicians and the leading cultural figures of the day. She was outside the mainstream in her social role – a single woman in a society which assumed that the 'natural' condition for a woman was to be a wife and mother – and, moreover, she was a single woman who lived alone (rather than with members of her family) on her own money. She was outside the mainstream in terms of her tastes: a woman with intellectual and literary interests in a society which regarded the appropriate concerns for a woman as familial and domestic. If it was the loss of her financially comfortable middle-class English home and its accompanying status that spurred her to publish *Miscellaneous Poems* when she was eighteen, it seems that the failure of her attempt to write specifically for middle-class English readers led to her decision to publish *Celtic Fables*. If her writing had been rejected by the mainstream English reading public, she would in turn reject them; she would write about Wales as English writers could not, and give Wales the book on its history which it deserved.

5

The Writing of History

Earlier phases of her authorial career show Williams responding in different genres to the same stimulus (*Artegall* and *Cambrian Tales* in response to the Blue Books) and exploring the variations possible within the same genre (the biography of Carnhuanawc, *The Paper People* and the 'autobiography' of Betsi Cadwaladr as varied examples of life writing). History had been one of her lifelong interests, as her early poems demonstrate, and in the last phase of her authorial career, history was the focus of her published writing in a variety of genres between 1869 and 1876: a book on the history of Wales, two articles on the respective histories of a place and a person, and a poem on a historical character.

The Literary Women of England had taken years of work on documentary material to produce a lengthy and detailed account of her subject which spanned hundreds of years; it had not been successful. Now, nearly sixty years old, she embarked on a new writing project, *A History of Wales derived from Authentic Sources*, which would also require her to spend years in detailed work on a wide range of documentary sources, and whose success was equally uncertain. Her biography of Carnhuanawc had suggested that he saw writing the history of Wales as a patriotic service; Williams may well have seen herself doing in English what he had done thirty years earlier in Welsh.

Her work on the book, however, would inevitably be affected by her failing health. Her chronic heart–lung condition had been formally diagnosed shortly after her move to London, but there are indications that it had affected her years earlier. In 1851, for example, when members of the Llanover house party went for a walk in the surrounding countryside, it was accepted that she would accompany them on horseback; she apparently did not have the energy to walk as far or as fast as the rest of the party.[1] This condition does not seem to have affected her when she was younger – looking after the Morgan children and acting as companion to Isabella Hughes would both have required physical energy, and her writing makes clear her personal knowledge of archaeological sites in Wales and Herefordshire which were reached only by energetic walking and climbing – but it became worse as she got older. In her 1871 grant application, when she was sixty-five, she describes herself as 'a sufferer from incurable maladies' who could barely walk 200 yards and was so badly affected by harsh winter weather that she was 'constantly confined to two rooms, and often to one'.[2] Even if she was describing the effects of her condition at their worst (and emphasising them for the purposes of the application), the state of her health would have had serious consequences for her energy and stamina; inevitably her work became more difficult as her health deteriorated. Taking on an ambitious writing project under these conditions could be seen as foolish, even foolhardy; it certainly indicated her belief in the project's importance and her faith that she would be able to bring it to a successful conclusion.

Writing the history of a country is inevitably a political act, a declaration that its people form a nation which is sufficiently different from others to have its own history, and that this history and this nation are worth writing about. In the nineteenth century, communities connected by geography and language (for example, in Italy and Germany) or embedded in larger states (in eastern Europe) regarded having their own written history as a statement that they were truly nations in their own right.[3] A national history had the task of describing the nation to itself as well as to others; to tell the story of one's own nation was to contribute towards building it.

To write a history of Wales was therefore to assert that Wales had an existence which was both significant and separate from that of England. Williams's book was published in London in a series which included histories of England (modern and medieval),

France and Greece, and of Ireland and India from the perspective of British settlers and administrators. The inclusion of *A History of Wales* in such a list was a declaration not only that Wales had its own distinctive history but that its history was as worth reading about as that of sovereign states. While her history had to present itself as objective in order to be regarded as trustworthy it inevitably reflected not only the values and assumptions of the period it was written in, but the values and assumptions (conscious or otherwise) of its author.[4]

Inevitably Welsh and English historians presented Welsh history differently. In the sixteenth century, for example, Humphrey Llwyd and David Powel both drew attention to the way Welsh culture and customs had been suppressed by English colonisers; in Powel's view, the effect had been to turn the Welsh people 'from civilitie to barbarisme'.[5] Later English historians, however, thought the exact opposite, reflecting a Whig view of history which saw it as a steady process of evolution, benignly controlled by those in power, which gradually spread social progress and prosperity.[6] William Warrington's *The History of Wales* (1786), for example, saw the conquest of Wales by Edward I as 'beneficial' to the Welsh because it taught them 'to polish their manners, to enlarge their views, and to cultivate their minds' – that is, to learn to think and behave like the English.[7] *Stories from the History of Wales* (1833), for children, explained that if Wales had not been conquered by the English, the Welsh people 'would not have enjoyed the ease, freedom and comfort that they do at the present day'.[8] B. B. Woodward's *The History of Wales* (1853) thought that Welsh history only began with the invading Saxons and that 'the extinction of the liberties of a brave [Welsh] people' was necessary to prevent Wales from 'being a perpetual hindrance to the great task which we see was allotted to the Saxons under the chieftainship of the Normans'; the extinction of Welsh liberties was mildly regrettable collateral damage in the achievement of the great Anglo-Saxon civilising mission.[9] In this view, the Welsh, their history, culture, language and literature, existed to serve the interests of England (and Matthew Arnold's lectures on Celtic literature argued that Wales's role – and the role of Celts in general – was to bring light, if not sweetness, to the English Philistines, and should be allowed to survive on those grounds alone).[10] Williams's account, by contrast, echoed Powel by declaring that 'In intellectual development, in literary culture and in social refinement the Welsh, as a people, excelled their conquerors'.[11]

Williams's book is very different from Carnhuanawc's *Hanes Cymru* – which, as his biographer, she knew well. Hers was in many ways the first attempt since Powel's in 1584 to write a history of Wales which did not rely on legends or the exploits of atypical individuals; instead it drew on 'modern' and 'scientific' views of what the study and writing of history should be. The Preface to her history discusses her sources in detail, and the only personal references appear in her explanation of her conclusions and methods: that when faced with conflicting evidence she consulted 'the best authorities' and listed her sources for the benefit of her readers, but expressed her 'own deliberate judgment' in the narrative.[12] While her reference to 'the best authorities' and the claim in her book's title that it was 'derived from Authentic Sources' assert that her history was grounded on these documentary sources, female historians faced a Catch-22; if they did not base their histories on the detailed information in their sources they were not 'real' historians, but if they did, their attention to detail demonstrated (in the words of Macaulay) that they were 'incapable of abstract reasoning'[13] – and in both cases (inevitably) inferior to their male rivals.

Williams chose not only to draw heavily on 'Authentic Sources' but to emphasise the fact. Although the lists of references are in smaller type than the main text, they occupy more than half the space of some pages and include not only sources one would expect (Caesar, Tacitus, Powel, Gibbon, Camden's *Britannia*, the *Myfyrian Archaeology*, the *Anglo-Saxon Chronicle*, William of Malmesbury, *Annales Cambriae*, Matthew Paris, and so on) but Herodotus, Aeschylus, Bacon, Milton, Spenser, Lyall's *Principles of Geology*, Sir Roderick Murchison's speech to the Cambrian Archaeological Society at Ludlow in 1852, and the Iolo Morganwg manuscripts.

It has been argued that because nineteenth-century historians of small nations embedded in larger ones were particularly anxious to avoid charges of writing partisan propaganda, they deliberately 'dissociated themselves from their subject-matter and acted as detached narrators'.[14] This is the exact opposite of Carnhuanawc's approach, but certainly true of Williams in *A History of Wales*; she used no first-person verbs or adjectives, did not address her readers directly, and the only reference to herself is oblique in both the grammatical and general senses. In an account of a line of first-century fortresses she mentions Tacitus's description of a battle site and the '[e]ntrenchments of Caer Caradog and Coxwall Knoll, situated upon the rugged height rising northward of the River Teme' and adds a footnote explaining that 'the ground has been personally explored by the author'; this is supported by seven documentary sources.[15] Her personal experience was clearly not enough on its own; it needed to be bolstered by a list of authoritative sources to be acceptable evidence. Any perceptible signs of personal bias could have led critics, reviewers and the increasing number of professional (male) historians to conclude that, like literature, serious academic history was, in the words of the reviewer of *The Literary Women of England*, 'no business for a woman'.

As if to counter any such suspicions, the first paragraph of *A History of Wales* demonstrates both intellectual rigour and a familiarity with contemporary anthropological theory:

> It has been well said that the memory of races, like that of individual men, tenaciously and vividly retains the recollections of infancy, which become in each race the subjects of oral traditions and of songs and ballads, until at last they assume a mythic or symbolic form, presenting two different aspects, one exhibiting the migrations of the several tribes and their arrival in successive colonies; the other assigning to each race a paternal ancestor, whose name personifies that of the people, and from whom an ethnological genealogy connects their tribes as his children and the kinsfolk of each other.[16]

The phrase 'ethnological genealogy' establishes a scholarly distance between Williams and her material; the early settlers of Britain are '*their* tribes' (for Carnhuanawc, by contrast, they are '*ein*' - ours). In this opening paragraph Williams uses analytical tools provided by the new and intellectually fashionable science of anthropology to construct a template, which she then applies to the Welsh founding myths; in the first 'aspect', according to Roman annals the ancestors of the Welsh came from Troy (the 'migration' of the tribe) and later arrived in Britain (the 'colony'). She follows this with another version which illustrates the second 'aspect', in which 'Brittus, called also Briutus or Bruttus' was a descendant of the biblical Japheth, became 'the progenitor of the Britons', and gave his name to their tribe (and since these two 'aspects' are contradictory, she leaves it to her readers to draw the obvious conclusion that they cannot both be true).[17]

Her treatment of these legends therefore declares that the Welsh are exactly like any other nation in having a founding myth – or (even better) two – and are thus able to meet international criteria for nation status. Just as Williams showed that the Welsh nation's founding myth(s) followed an established template, so she showed that the effects on it of contacts with another nation – the Romans (contacts that included military conquest, social, cultural and linguistic influences, and intermarriage) – also followed the standard pattern. In this too her attitude contrasted with Carnhuanawc's, and the difference between their approaches is revealing.

This contrast is not surprising; the treatment of the Roman invasion and occupation of Britain had divided historians in previous centuries also. The eighteenth century, for example, saw two books on this subject published within eight years of each other under the same title, *Britannia Romana*; the first (by John Pointer) praised 'our Renown'd and Warlike Ancestors, the bold Britains [*sic*]', simultaneously thanking the Romans for 'beating them into Civility, Learning and good Manners: so that we their successors may be bold to say, we are now become the most civiliz'd Nation in the World', while the second (by John Horsley) was written entirely from the perspective of the Romans, calling the Roman army in Britain 'the British army' and referring to the inhabitants of Britain themselves as 'the enemy' throughout.[18] Whereas to Carnhuanawc, like Pointer, the early inhabitants of Britain were 'our ancestors', 'our forefathers' and – revealingly – 'our tribe',[19] for Williams they were 'them'. To Carnhuanawc the Roman army was a terrible ravening wild beast with iron teeth; to Williams it was a force for order which created social stability for the indigenous community.[20] He saw the remains of Roman roads as scars on the face of Wales and reminders of its subjection to the conquerors; Williams pointed out that the roads built by the Roman army for military purposes also benefited civilians.[21] She listed (exhaustively) the range of fruit, vegetables, domestic animals and birds which the Romans had brought to Britain, emphasising that these imports had literally become part of the Welsh landscape and of everyday Welsh life.[22]

To Carnhuanawc the Romans were foreign oppressors; to Williams a foreign occupation could have beneficial consequences if the occupiers established the conditions necessary for a peaceful civil society.[23] To Carnhuanawc, the Welsh of his day were exactly the same as the Ancient Britons who had lived in Wales before the Roman invasion; they lived in the same territory, spoke the same language (allowing for inevitable modifications over the centuries) and shared the same (pure) bloodlines; to him, the superficial effects of the Roman conquest were easily reversed once the occupation ended. To Williams, by contrast, major events in Welsh history such as the Roman occupation inevitably changed the Welsh people and the way they lived their lives, and contributed to what they became over the following centuries; like other nations they had a many-stranded inheritance and a correspondingly complex national identity. Her acceptance of this complexity allows for a much more sophisticated treatment than Carnhuanawc's.

The choice and presentation of material in *A History of Wales* inevitably reveal its author's opinions. Just as her account of Roman rule in Wales shows clearly her own views on the role of government and the nature of national identity, so the book as a whole makes obvious her religious beliefs and prejudices. She was a devout Anglican, and for her the Church of England represented 'true religion'. She was very aware that as an Anglican in Wales she was a member of a minority; her writing on the Anglican Church in

Wales often strikes a defensive note, and, like many others then and in previous centuries, she blamed failings in the Anglican hierarchy for the growth of Nonconformism in Wales. English bishops were appointed to Welsh sees and in turn appointed to Welsh livings Englishmen who knew no Welsh and saw no reason to learn it; the complaint that the Anglican Church in Wales suffered from 'the want of Pastors who understand the language' (in the words of Evan Evans in the mid-eighteenth century) was historic and perennial.[24] The result was that Welsh-speakers were drawn to worship at Nonconformist services conducted in Welsh and led by ministers closer to them in social class and culture than middle-class English clerics.[25] Her concern was entirely justified: the 'Religious Census' of 1851 recorded that only 20 per cent of worshippers in Wales attended Anglican places of worship, while more than 75 per cent attended those of Baptist, Independent and Methodist (Calvinistic Methodists, at more than 25 per cent, on their own outnumbered Anglicans).[26]

Williams's strongest animosity, however, was directed at the Roman Catholic Church – an animosity which had been ingrained in Welsh society since at least the seventeenth century.[27] In the nineteenth century anti-Catholicism was particularly powerful in rural areas (which saw far fewer real live Roman Catholics than the cities)[28]. This antipathy was deeply irrational – only 0.8 per cent of the population of Wales attended Roman Catholic places of worship in Wales – but very powerful; Williams fully shared the powerful anti-Catholic prejudices of most of the population of Wales, and this paranoia is reflected in both *The Autobiography of Elizabeth Davis* and *The Literary Women of England*. In *A History of Wales* it distorts to a remarkable degree Williams's judgement on the crucial turning-point in Welsh history.

For most historians of Wales – 'modern' nineteenth-century ones as well as earlier chroniclers – the death of Llywelyn ap Gruffydd in 1282 was a watershed, and the point at which the 'truly Welsh' history of Wales ended in the loss of national independence. To Williams, however, the death of Llywelyn ap Gruffydd was merely one of a series of events in medieval Welsh history – sad and significant, but not crucial. After her account of Llywelyn's death she recounts how 'the wise and sagacious King Edward' made his infant son the Prince of Wales, and presents Welsh history in the late thirteenth century as moving in a measured, coherent and unbroken line.[29] The reason for this becomes clear three chapters (and more than 250 years) later; for Williams the pivotal process in Welsh history was not the obliteration of the line of the princes of Gwynedd, with all its political, military, social, literary and cultural consequences, but the Protestant Reformation.

She had prepared readers for this by her criticism of the medieval Church: she declared that Norman prelates 'darkened, hardened and embittered the minds of the Welsh', that Pope Calixtus II offered the Welsh clergy 'superstitious and mercenary incentives' to accept his authority and, while praising some individual churchmen for their piety and honesty, refused to take others seriously. Rhydderch Hael, for example, became a monk 'in a superstitious panic', while Giraldus Cambrensis behaved in a way that showed 'utter ignorance of real piety', demonstrated 'mortified vanity', and failed to be appointed bishop of St David's because the successful candidate 'was a quiet man and Giraldus was not'.[30] She also criticised the way in which secular rulers tried to manipulate the Church for their own ends, including Henry VII's 'superstitious' attempt to have his predecessor and enemy Henry VI canonised 'to enhance his own importance'.[31] Her treatment of his son, Henry VIII, however, is very different; her account develops into a full-throated paean of praise, entirely because of his effect on organised religion in Wales: 'For deliverance from the domination of the Pope of Rome, and for the suppression of the monasteries, England and Wales stand for ever indebted to the fiercely resolute will of Henry VIII.'[32]

She does not discuss the reasons for Henry VIII's break from Rome, and she clearly had no illusions that he himself became a Protestant or was sympathetic to Protestant doctrines; in her account of the life of Anne Askew in *The Literary Women of England*, Williams makes it clear that Henry VIII's rejection of 'the domination of the Pope of Rome' lay entirely in his repudiation of papal authority, that he regarded 'many of the genuine doctrines of the Reformation' as 'heresy' and that he was responsible for a law which established the death penalty for those who denied Roman Catholic doctrines.[33] Williams did not see Henry VIII as a defender of Protestantism but rather as a bigoted and ignorant instrument of the divine will, God's useful idiot. In her eyes Henry VIII's role in establishing Protestantism in England and Wales was so momentous that it even outweighed his 'lamentable mistake' of the 'language clause' in the 1536 Act of Union, which by excluding the use of Welsh from courts of law and all other official administrative functions 'instituted a grievance which has been felt through many following generations'.[34] Even this, however, was of less importance than his role in establishing Protestantism and 'the divine power of scriptural truth' in Wales.

For many Welsh people 'the divine power of scriptural truth' was only accessible after the Bible had been translated into Welsh, and Williams devotes several pages of the book's last chapter to the first full translation in 1588, crediting the clerics responsible for translating different sections of the Bible and describing the conditions in which they worked. This level of detail, however, makes an important omission particularly noticeable: her history ignores the fact that neither the Act of Parliament which ordered the translation nor the command of the Privy Council that all Welsh parishes should buy a copy before Christmas 1588 could have happened without the approval of Elizabeth I.[35] Given Williams's understanding of the centrality of the Welsh Bible to religion in Wales (she describes it as 'an inestimable treasure'), it is revealing that she merely refers to Elizabeth in a subordinate phrase – 'Elizabeth being queen' at the time the translation was made – rather than praising her role in the Welsh Bible's production as she had praised Henry VIII's role in the Protestant Reformation.[36] The probable reason can be found in the section on Elizabeth in *The Literary Women of England*, in which Williams attacked both the queen's personality (accusing her of 'elaborate duplicity') and her poetry: 'The tone is heathen and the spirit malevolent.'[37] Clearly Williams had made up her mind about Elizabeth I before she came to write her *History of Wales*;

she was happy to praise Henry VIII's role in establishing Protestantism in Wales while criticising his personal religious beliefs, but not to give his daughter credit for her role in establishing Welsh as the language of religion in Wales. In spite of Williams's attempts to position herself as an objective narrator of the facts derived from 'Authentic Sources', her *History of Wales* (inevitably) exhibits just as much personal bias as the work of any other historian.

A History of Wales was a major project which dominated Williams's life for more than four years; given the precarious state of her health, its successful conclusion was a remarkable achievement. Its final paragraph communicates an almost palpable relief that the end of the work was in sight, and a confidence that Welsh history had ended happily ever after:

> Under the influence of gentler and more equitable treatment than the nation ever experienced before the accession of their Henry, and under the divine power of Scriptural truth, Wales has gradually become a land of peace, to which bloodshed with heinous crime in every form is now almost unknown.[38]

At the end of a book which described in detail cruelty, oppression, murder and tortures throughout the centuries, the book ends with a Panglossian certainty that everything in the course of Welsh history was for the best, in the best of all possible worlds.

The combination of her demanding work on *A History of Wales* – not only the laborious revision of successive handwritten drafts of a lengthy book, but correcting multiple versions of the proofs – and her deteriorating health seem to have made Williams aware that the time left for her to write, and see her writings through the press, might be limited and that she should deal with any unfinished business as soon as possible. Years earlier she had received research material from two people who had been important to her; writing and publishing articles based on the papers they had entrusted to her became a priority. The first article to be published used documents she had received from Isabella Hughes more than twenty-five years earlier.

'Some Particulars of the Parish of Glasbury in the Counties of Brecknock and Radnor obtained from authentic documents, local tradition, books and personal observation' was published in *Archaeologia Cambrensis* in 1870, and its lengthy title is pedantically precise; it does not pretend to offer a history of Glasbury, but merely to present some details which relate to it. The 'authentic documents' form its main source material, occupying more than half the article's pages, and internal evidence shows that they had belonged to the Rev. John Hughes of Glasbury, Isabella's father.

The article contains no introduction, no conclusion, and no attempt to structure the information into a narrative; the documents are merely transcribed and presented without authorial comment. They are of strictly local interest, and include detailed accounts of parish boundaries and a petition from parishioners to the bishop in 1665 to build a new church to replace one damaged by flood. The purpose of the article was apparently to put the documents' contents in the public domain; Williams was a copyist rather than an author.

The second article used material collected and passed to her by her eldest brother, Henry David, more than forty years earlier; in contrast to the first, it makes her personal preoccupations very clear, and her emotional involvement in her subject is explicit in its title. 'An Account of Henry Williams of Ysgafell in the Parish of Llanllwchaiarn and County of Montgomeryshire, by his descendant Jane Williams' was published in 1871 in the *Transactions of the Powys-Land Club*: that is, in a journal of local history rather than one with the Wales-wide circulation of *Archaeologia Cambrensis*.

The Paper People shows that Jane and her eldest brother, Henry David, had been close as children and that this closeness continued into adulthood; surviving family papers show that, like her, Henry was deeply interested in family history (especially as it related to himself).[39] He had been a lieutenant in the British army, and in this article Jane Williams refers to him not only as 'the late lineal descendant of the Williamses of Ysgafell' but as 'of Her Majesty's 54th and 26th regiments'. He had transferred from the 54th Regiment of Foot to the 26th only six weeks before his death, and his children's later references to him place him still in the 54th when he died. The fact that Williams included in her article the irrelevant fact of his army service, and that she remembered details of his regiments correctly, suggests that thirty years after his death he remained important to her.[40]

Henry Williams of Ysgafell, who lived from the 1620s to 1684, was a friend and protégé of Vavasour Powell, Baptist minister and Fifth Monarchy Man. Like Powell he was persecuted by the authorities after the restoration of the monarchy in 1660 because he continued to preach and hold services without a licence – unobtainable because he could not in conscience accept the 1662 revisions to the Anglican Book of Common Prayer or take the Oath of Supremacy. Contemporary accounts (quoted by Jane Williams) show that near-miraculous stories like those told of medieval saints had become attached to his name, and for some later historians he became the epitome of a Puritan who suffered under penal laws after the Restoration.[41] Williams's account shows that she admired Henry Williams's willingness to suffer hardship and persecution for the sake of his conscience, that she hoped that she would have shown equal fortitude, and that she was proud to be his descendant. In contrast to the 'objective' truths she had aimed for in *A History of Wales* and her role as an impersonal conduit of information in 'Some Particulars of the Parish of Glasbury', in this article her obvious emotional involvement with her subject completely overwhelms her critical judgement.

No writing by Henry Williams of Ysgafell survived, but Williams makes the reasonable assumption that he shared Powell's religious and political views – reasonable, because since Powell's writings show his conviction that he was completely right about everything, always, it is difficult to imagine that he would have been as close to Henry Williams as he clearly was if Henry Williams's views had in any way diverged from his own.[42] Williams's bibliography for the article shows that she had read extensively in Powell's writings as well as about him, which makes her entirely inaccurate statement that '[Powell's and Henry Williams's] confession of faith agreed with the doctrinal articles of the Church of England' very revealing;

if Powell and Henry Williams had been able to accept the 'doctrinal articles of the Church of England' they would have been able to make the declarations necessary to obtain a licence to preach, and therefore would not have fallen foul of the authorities. Even more strikingly, Williams then summarises their religious beliefs (*for* adult baptism, spontaneous prayers, civil and religious liberty and republican institutions; *against* infant baptism, set forms of worship, tithes, bishops, and the monarchy) which directly contradicted those same doctrinal articles of the Church of England she had just declared they accepted.[43] She cannot have been oblivious to the fact.

Just as she wanted to think that Henry Williams's beliefs were essentially Anglican like hers – in spite of all the evidence which disproved it – so she wanted to believe that stories told about him were literally true in spite of documentary proof to the contrary. An anecdote (which had achieved legendary status in the area) told how, after soldiers sent by magistrates had taken his animals and his harvested crops and destroyed the crops growing in his fields, his family's survival depended on the one field which the soldiers had neglected to lay waste. Later in the year, at harvest time, other farmers in the area reported average crops, but this field – and this field alone – produced wheat with double and triple ears, which 'astonished the country' and was regarded as a sign of divine favour. The field became known locally as 'Cae Bendith', the Field of Blessing, and when Henry David Williams visited the area more than 150 years later, local people were still able to identify the 'miraculous' field.[44] Jane Williams's treatment of this story shows that she needed it to be literally true rather than just an engaging folk tale; by reading botanical histories she identified the variety of 'miraculous' wheat which transformed her ancestor's fortunes in the 1680s – but then discovered that it had not been introduced into Britain until 1799. Given her merciless attacks on factual impossibilities in her earlier writings, that should have been the point at which she abandoned any suggestion that the story was literally true. Instead, she made the following remarkable comment:

> [The multiple-eared wheat's] sudden and abundant appearance at Ysgafell more than a century earlier, to persons ignorant of the very existence of such a species must, therefore, have been surprising, and might reasonably under the circumstances be attributed to an especial Providence.[45]

Williams was careful to the point of pedantry in her choice of language, and the first half of this sentence implies that a variety of wheat unknown in Britain until 1799 did indeed 'appear' at Ysgafell in the 1680s. Her readers were apparently being asked to believe that, of all the fields in all the farms in all the counties of England and Wales, that particular variety of wheat happened to manifest itself in the one undamaged field on her ancestor's farm not only at the exact moment when its arrival would make the most difference, but at a moment when its presence was physically impossible. To interpret ambiguous or fragmentary evidence in her ancestor's favour would have been one thing; to contradict 'Authentic Sources' was a serious offence against the principles on which she had proudly based her other historical writings. It reflects both her pride in an ancestor who figured in Welsh history and the importance to her of her connection with a piece of the land of Wales – even if none of her family had lived there for more than 150 years or owned it for nearly a century and even if (as her article suggests) she herself had never been there. The intellectual rigour, careful critical judgement and the determination to be guided by 'Authentic Sources' which her other historical writings show had melted into air in the face of emotional imperatives more powerful than intellectual or scholarly ones.

In 1876 Williams entered a poem in competition at the Wrexham Eisteddfod (at this period some of the Eisteddfod's activities were held in English); the competition title was 'Owain Lawgoch'. Over fifty years earlier, her poem 'A Welsh Bard's Lamentation', on the death of Llywelyn ap Gruffydd, had shown how an event from medieval Welsh history could spark her imagination into poetry when it had some parallels with her own situation; the title for the eisteddfod poem had the same effect on her in 1876. The story of the descendant of a prominent family who had his birthright taken from him, who went to live in another country, was active in one of the few occupations open to him and who became widely known and respected through the skilful use of his talents was close enough to aspects of her own life story to allow her to feel she could identify with his situation; the fact that Owain's family history, career and death were considerably more dramatic (and violent) than her own was less important than the similarities. Her poem came second in the competition.

As she moved into her mid-seventies it must have seemed that the rest of her life would be dominated by poor health and an inadequate income, but when she was seventy-seven the latter problem was eased; she inherited substantial investments from her sister Elizabeth (they came ultimately from their maternal grandfather and great-uncle, William and Robert Marsh, via their maternal aunt Elizabeth and their sister Eleanor[46]). She made a new will in response to her changed financial circumstances; Elizabeth's will had made it clear that she saw these investments as family property which as far as possible should be passed on to the next generation, and Jane Williams left the bulk of her assets to be shared equally among her nephews and nieces (even though she could not remember the names of all of them[47]). A small proportion of her new-found wealth, however, went to pay another moral debt.

Her maid, Mary Willey, a Scotswoman from Inverness-shire, had worked for her for many years – for inadequate wages because Williams's limited income had not allowed her to pay the standard rate. Williams left Willey not only her household linen, crockery and cutlery (and, with typically practical consideration, 'suitable Boxes Baskets and Bags for their safe removal') but some shares and the income from a rented-out workshop (both inherited from Elizabeth) in gratitude for 'the underpaid varied disinterested and valuable service' she had given over the years.[48] When Williams made her will, Mary Willey was in her late sixties and had not been able to save for her old age because Williams could not afford to pay her adequately; the bequest, while not particularly generous, should have meant that after Williams's death Willey would not be faced with the prospect of physical drudgery until she became too old and weak and had to end her days in the workhouse. The bequest should also have meant that over time she would gradually be able to save enough money to be buried decently and avoid the horrors of a pauper's burial.

But life – and death – frustrated these plans. In the last weeks of Jane Williams's life, when the relentless progress of her illness would have made it clear she would not live much longer, Mary Willey was diagnosed with terminal cancer; it was clear that while she would outlive Williams, she would not survive for long enough to receive enough income from Williams's legacy to pay for a decent burial. When she died, five months after Williams, she was buried in Williams's grave in Brompton Cemetery, Chelsea[49] (it would be interesting to know if Williams had considered being buried in Wales). The burial in the same grave of two people not connected by blood or marriage and of different social classes is sufficiently unusual to suggest that in the last weeks of her life Jane Williams told her executors to have Willey buried in the same grave rather than expose her to a pauper's burial, a reflection of the gratitude her will expresses to a woman who had been her 'excellent personal attendant and faithful servant and attached friend'.[50] It seems unlikely that her executors would have arranged for this without her explicit instructions.

Williams herself died on 16 March 1885; the 'dilation and defective action' of her heart finally prevailed. Her will instructed her executors (a friend and a niece) to 'carefully and conscientiously preserve' her copies of her published works 'together with all my literary manuscripts note books pocket books letters and written papers of every kind' until a descendant of her maternal grandparents should 'manifestly prove to be capable of rightly valuing using and transmitting them'.[51] It seems that she may have been hoping that one of these descendants would either write her biography themselves or pass on her papers to someone who would; it also seems that no member of her family had 'manifestly' demonstrated themselves to be suitable for the task during her lifetime and that, judging by the fact that her papers were dispersed and mainly lost, no such person emerged later. Only a few of the papers mentioned in her will are now in the public domain, and it is impossible to guess at what the others might have contained. Judging by the quality of those that have survived, the others would have made interesting reading.

In her writing as in her life Jane Williams carved out her own path for herself. To write and publish for more than fifty years, and in a wide range of genres, would be a considerable achievement for any author; to do so as a woman in the second and third quarters of the nineteenth century presented an even greater challenge, and required great determination and considerable self-confidence. Williams was a female author whose writing focused on 'serious and laborious' subjects which many people considered inappropriate for a woman; she did not marry or have children, and lived independently in a period when general opinion regarded this as flying in the face of 'Nature'. Williams clearly had to be a strong-minded woman – in the modern, if not the nineteenth-century, sense – to live the life she did and achieve as much as she did. Her life and literary career are remarkable.

She was not alone as a woman writing in English who spread her literary talents over a wide range of genres, of course: Elizabeth Gaskell (1810–65) wrote novels, biographies, poems, short stories, articles and reviews; Margaret Oliphant (1828–87), who also wrote novels, biographies and literary histories and articles, had in addition enough French and Italian to review books in both languages; Eliza Meteyard (1816–79), who wrote novels, biography, histories, short stories and children's books, was also known for her journalism; Sara Coleridge (1802–52) wrote fantasy novels and poetry for children as well as translations from Latin and French; Jean Ingelow (1820–97) wrote poems, novels, and children's stories;[52] Jameson and Costello have already been mentioned. Williams, however, worked in a wider range of genres and had a longer writing career than any of them.

Another obvious contrast between Williams and the writers mentioned above is that most of her published work related to Wales; here it is the range of genres in which she worked that sets her apart. Women authors with Welsh connections and subjects who wrote in English during the same period were considerably more limited in their range of genres: Felicia Hemans (1793–1835) and Maria James (1795–*c*.1848) were poets; Ann Julia Hatton (1764–1838) and Anne Beale (1816–1900) wrote poetry and novels; Angharad Llwyd (1780–1866) was a historian; Lady Charlotte Guest (1812–95) a translator. (It was not until later in the century that women such as Cranogwen and Moelona worked in a wider range of genres, and they did so in Welsh.)[53] It is the combination of factors – that she, a woman, had a writing career of over half a century *and* wrote in a wide range of genres *and* that much of her writing was serious non-fiction *and* that she wrote in English about Wales and matters Welsh – that makes her unique.

This combination of factors means that she resists easy classification, and her life and work are full of apparent contradictions. Her writing shows a detailed and scholarly knowledge of literary and historical sources in four languages (English, Welsh, French, Latin), but her formal education ended when she was fourteen. She spent most of her life in England (approximately forty-five of her seventy-nine years), but wrote most successfully on Welsh subjects. She regretted that she had not been born in Wales, but when she visited London after thirty years away she enjoyed breathing her 'native air' again.[54]

She could write about Wales from the perspective of someone who knew well the Welsh people, landscape, history, literature, language and culture but who was not of Wales in the same sense as people who lived their whole lives there; in England, where she chose to live for the last thirty years of her life, she could assume the perspective of someone who knew well the English people, landscape, history, language, literature and culture but was also not fully of it, because of the formative years she had spent in Wales. Whichever of the two she located herself in at any given moment, she could not help but be aware of the other: 'Ynom mae'r clawdd' ('Offa's Dyke – the border – is within us') wrote Bryan Martin Davies.[55] To the Royal Literary Fund she described herself as Welsh 'by descent and long residence'; she could equally well have described herself as English by the same criteria. She was of both countries and cultures yet not completely of either, a hybrid who made her hybridity into an advantage, using the freedom it gave her to construct the personal and literary identities she chose for herself. In the process of crossing and recrossing boundaries and borders – national, social, financial, literary, linguistic and cultural – she carved out a unique position for herself.

Certainly Wales – its landscape, its people, its history, language, literature and culture – inspired, enthused, intrigued and amused her from the earliest of her published work to her last, and most of her writing in between. An equally pervasive element in her writing is a sense of loss – and, with an irony she may well have appreciated, it was through a life-changing loss (of her family's money and social status when she was in her teens) that she gained the knowledge and experience of Wales and matters Welsh which became so important to her. She had been brought up and educated to think of herself as middle-class, and her cultural and literary interests were very much those of the class she had been born into, but the practical and financial circumstances of her life meant that her membership of this social class could never be unproblematic. She later moved among the rich and famous, aristocrats and diplomats, who she felt treated her as an equal; but her social position was always precarious, and her financial position so dire that she resorted to an elaborate stratagem to give the illusion of dressing appropriately. Her family had come down in the world, and the descent turned out to be permanent; any hopes that one or all of her three brothers would restore the family fortunes faded and died.[56]

It is no coincidence that a sense of loss – irrevocable, life-changing, a gap which can never be filled – lies beneath even her lightest and most entertaining pieces of writing (the comedy in *Cambrian Tales*, the lighter poems in *Celtic Fables*) and her sardonic comments in *Artegall*, the biography of Carnhuanawc, *The Literary Women of*

England and *A History of Wales*. Further, a deep sense of loss is the focus of some of her most personal writing: 'Sink not my Soul', 'Lines on the Banks of the Llunvey' and 'A Welsh Bard's Lamentation for the Death of the Last Llewellyn [*sic*] Prince of Wales' from *Miscellaneous Poems*; *The Paper People*; most of the poems in *Celtic Fables*, especially 'Elidwr'; her essay on Henry Williams of Ysgafell. Indeed, the effects of the loss of the Ysgafell estate also echo throughout her writing life, symbolised by her decision to choose it as her bardic name. It seems that in some ways she tried to treat Neuadd Felen in Talgarth as a substitute; in her will (made in 1883) she described herself as 'late of Neuadd Felen', although by that time she had not lived there for nearly three decades, no member of her family had lived there for more than eight years, and her family had never owned it.

The uncertainties and insecurities which permeated so many aspects of her life meant that her identity as a writer was doubly important to her. Circumstances beyond her control meant that until she was nearly forty she was unable to write and publish as she wished; when events combined to free her from these constraints she appreciated the opportunities her new life gave her, and made the most of them with extra enjoyment because she knew very well that they might not have happened. Her reworking of the Aesop fable – written and published for her own interest and enjoyment – is particularly revealing; after her failure to make money with *The Literary Women of England* she did not aim at commercial success with another Ant-like project but followed the promptings of her inner Grasshopper, writing and publishing what she wanted to though aware that the result might be financial failure. As she wrote sardonically to the Royal Literary Fund to explain why she needed to ask for financial help, 'the very titles' of her published works show that 'the desire to make money' was not her 'prevalent motive in writing them' – or, as Geraldine Jewsbury wrote bluntly in support of Williams's application, 'Her works do not sell.'[57]

Williams's 'prevalent motive' for writing was that she *needed* to write; her response to anything which moved her deeply – the loss of the family money and status, the loss of Ysgafell, the Blue Books, a childhood game and the happiness it represented, Welsh fables and legends, Welsh history – was to write about it. Other things, and many people, came and went in her life; she moved from one country to another, one social class to another, one culture to another and one genre to another, but throughout those changes one thing was constant. The writing remained.

Appendix I

Jane Williams's Birthplace and Early Life

Relatively little documentation has survived about Jane Williams's early life, and much of the information generally available about her is inaccurate or misleading.

Her Place of Birth

In her application to the Royal Literary Fund, Williams said she had been born in Chelsea; at the time of her birth her parents were living at 35 Sloane Square, and she was baptised at St Luke's, Chelsea's parish church. When she visited London from Wales for the first time in nearly thirty years, she wrote of the pleasure of breathing 'her native air' again.[1]

However, the first account of her life and work, in Edwin Poole's *History of Breconshire* (1886), described her as a 'native' of the Talgarth 'neighbourhood' and 'a truly native-born Breconian', and this has influenced some later writers (for example, Theophilus Jones and Matthew Owen). Poole added that she 'spent a greater part of her life at Aberllynfi and at Neuadd Felen, Talgarth';[2] he gave no sources for these statements. When the Williams family moved to Breconshire they lived first at Aberenig House which at that time was outside Talgarth, and so 'in the Talgarth neighbourhood'. It is impressive enough that Poole's informant(s) remembered that nearly fifty years earlier an unremarkable family had moved to Neuadd Felen *in* Talgarth from a house *outside* it; it is not surprising that they did not know (or remember) that more than fifteen years earlier the family had moved to Aberenig House from somewhere else. The matter is further confused when later writers miss Poole's distinction between the Williams family living first in the Talgarth 'neighbourhood' and later 'in' Talgarth itself at Neuadd Felen, and describe Jane Williams as living at Neuadd Felen *near* Talgarth;[3] Neuadd Felen is very definitely *in* Talgarth, roughly equidistant between the main square and the parish church. Poole's reference to Williams living at Aberllynfi probably refers to her time as Isabella Hughes's companion at Aberllunvey House.

The entry on Jane Williams in the 1900 edition of the *Dictionary of National Biography* was the first reference book to give Chelsea as her place of birth – but in Riley Street rather than Sloane Square.[4] (This information is most likely to have come from Jane Williams's last surviving sibling, her youngest sister Mary Ann, who would have remembered Riley Street but not Sloane Square as the family home in Chelsea when she was a small child.) Research done on Maxwell Fraser's behalf in the Chelsea Poor Rate Tax books discovered that the Williams family did not move to Riley Street until Jane Williams was eleven years old, but this has not discouraged some writers from continuing to say that she was born there.[5]

Her Early Life

Where Jane Williams spent her early life and especially when she first went to live in the Glasbury–Talgarth area of Breconshire has been even more contentious; again, Williams herself provides valuable information. In *Artegall* (written in 1847) she claimed 'more than twenty years' experience of the Moral and Physical Condition of the [Welsh] people' – a subject on which *Artegall* attacked the Commissioners' ignorance.[6] While 'more than' is vague, her remark clearly indicates that she had first come to know 'the Moral and Physical Condition' of the Welsh people in the early or mid-1820s: that is, when the Preface and poems in *Miscellaneous Poems* (1824) show she was living in Glasbury. Her comment asserts her knowledge of Welsh rural life in contrast to the Commissioners' ignorance of it, so that the longer she had lived in rural Wales, the stronger her case would have been. If she had been able to say that her experience of Welsh rural society had been longer than 'more than twenty years' this is a context in which she would certainly have done so.

Williams's own words, therefore, directly contradict the accounts in several reference books that she spent 'the first half of her life' in Neuadd Felen, Talgarth; some writers say that her family moved to live in Talgarth when she was a small child.[7] Others realise that since her father worked for the Navy Office (stated in the 1900 *DNB*) he would not have lived in Talgarth, since it is many miles from the sea and any naval base; they state or imply that her childhood was spent in Talgarth because of her 'weak health'[8] – apparently so severe that it required her to live apart from her parents and siblings. There is certainly evidence of weak health, the result of the heart–lung condition, in the later part of her life, but her employment with the Morgans and Isabella Hughes in her teens, twenties and thirties does not suggest serious health problems, while her references to going up Cader Idris and exploring 'rugged heights' in the countryside near Clifford also indicate that 'weak health' was not a significant factor in her life when she was young.[9]

The available evidence, therefore, gives no reason to think that she and her family were living in the Glasbury–Talgarth area before the early 1820s, when she was in her mid-teens.

Appendix 2

The Authorship of *Twenty Essays*

Essays I–VI are very different from Jane Williams's writings in their treatment of their subjects, organisation of material and especially in style. The contrasts between these six essays and Essays XII–XX, which share characteristics with her other writings, are best illustrated by examples. From the first six essays:

> Those sacred conceptions of evil which have lurked within or produced open sin, those instances of resistance to the awakening voice of Providence, and to the Holy Spirit's influences, those multiplied mercies which make ingratitude in his [the sinner's] case so black a crime, and that peculiar sense of God's loving kindness, and of personal obligation, which render him an offender against knowledge, his desertion of feelings and faculties which he had consecrated to the service of his Lord, these things, but with a power unutterable by human tongue, teach the true penitent's heart, when returning he renews his application to the Saviour's blood, that his offences are more heinous than those of other men, that he is indeed the chief of sinners.[1]

And from the last eight:

> Speech is a medium of communicating our wants and wishes, of relating what has happened to us, of expressing our pains and pleasures, and of asking for sympathy. It commands, entreats, consoles and delights us. It instructs in matters of fact and experience, in worldly, intellectual and spiritual knowledge. It tells of courtesy, and kindness, and affection, and conduces to the happiness of social life.[2]

The first extract – one sentence – is structurally complex and its accumulation of clauses is confusing to navigate on first reading.

The second uses a series of structurally simple clauses which make the writer's meaning immediately clear.

There are also considerable discrepancies in the contents and approach of the two groups of essays. It is difficult to believe that Williams was the author of a comment in one of the first essays which refers slightingly to women's intellectual abilities and interests, for example, and the two groups contain mutually incompatible judgements: essays in the first group demonstrate social and intellectual snobbery ('The multitude have low notions and . . . perverted ambition') while the second group express far more egalitarian – even humble – opinions ('Everyone knows something, and most people know many things better than ourselves').[3] While the essays in the first group are remarkably humourless, Essay XV remarks sardonically that the number of published books strikes 'some people, who love them not, with alarm', while Essay XVIIII comments that boring people 'try their hearers' patience with tedious traditional histories and oracular judgments, while exciting pity for the folly of which these things are outward demonstrations'.[4]

The only satisfactory explanation for the marked differences between the two groups of essays at the levels of content, approach to and organisation of their material, and sentence structure is that they were written by different people. The second group shares characteristics at these levels with Williams's later writings, while the first group emphatically does not.

Notes

I

1. St Luke's Chelsea PR.
2. See Gwyneth Tyson Roberts, '"The fair sequester'd vale": Two Early Poems of Place by Jane Williams (Ysgafell)', *The International Journal of Welsh Writing in English*, II (Cardiff: University of Wales Press, 2014) for a detailed account of the house's location.
3. See Judith Johnston, *Anna Jameson: Victorian, Feminist, Woman of Letters* (Aldershot: Scolar Press, 1997), and Clare Broome Saunders, *Louisa Stuart Costello: A Nineteenth-Century Writing Life* (Basingstoke: Palgrave Macmillan, 2015).
4. Johnston, *Anna Jameson*, pp. 3–4.
5. Saunders, *Louisa Stuart Costello*, p. 10.
6. RLF MS, pp. 6, 8.
7. See Peter Lord, *Words with Pictures: Welsh Images and Images of Wales in the Popular Press, 1640–1860* (Aberystwyth: Planet, 1995), pp. 34, 37, 130; Moira Dearnley, *Distant Fields: Eighteenth-Century Fictions of Wales* (Cardiff: University of Wales Press, 2001), pp. xiii, xvi; W. J. Hughes, *Wales and the Welsh in English Literature from Shakespeare to Scott* (Wrexham, London: Hughes & Son, 1924), *passim*; Tyson Roberts, 'Two Early Poems of Place by Jane Williams (Ysgafell)', (1998, 2011); and, for a blast of Anglocentric anti-Welsh bile accumulated over the centuries, T. W. H. Crosland, *Taffy was a Welshman* (London: Ewart, Seymour & Co., 1912), *passim*.
8. Jane Williams's will (made 24 October 1883, proved 28 March 1885).
9. After her death, her niece and executor Eleanor Marsh Williams took charge of her papers. A small group of these was acquired by the National Library of Wales in April 2014 (NLW MS 24051F); apparently nothing more is known of any of the documents mentioned in Jane Williams's will.

[10] T. R. Roberts, *Eminent Welshmen*, vol. I (Cardiff and Merthyr Tydfil: The Educational Publishing Company, 1908), p. 565 and *D W B*, pp. 1044–5; Theophilus Jones, *A History of the County of Brecknock in Two Volumes* (1805–9; Brecknock: Edwin Davies, 1898), p. 50; Meic Stephens (ed.) *The Oxford Companion to the Literature of Wales* (Oxford: Oxford University Press, 1986), p. 778.

[11] Deborah C. Fisher, *Who's Who in Welsh History* (Swansea: Christopher Davies, 1997), p. 157; see also *The Rhondda Leader*, 10 November 1906, p. 2, both of which confuse Ysgafell with Maria Jane Williams (Llinos), and Peter Bell, *Victorian Women: An Index to Biographies and Memoirs* (Edinburgh: P. Bell, *c.*1989, no pagination), which confuses her with Jane Williams, wife of Edward.

[12] Nigel Cross, *The Common Writer: Life in Nineteenth-Century Grub Street* (Cambridge: Cambridge University Press, 1985), pp. 167–8.

[13] See Jane Aaron, *Pur fel y Dur: Y Gymraes yn Llên Menywod y Bedwaredd Ganrif ar Bymtheg* (Caerdydd: Gwasg Prifysgol Cymru, 1998); *Nineteen-Century Women's Writing in Wales: Nation, Gender and Identity* (Cardiff: University of Wales Press, 2007), and Katie Gramich and Catherine Brennan (eds), *Welsh Women's Poetry 1460–2001* (Dinas Powys: Honno, 2003).

[14] RLF MS, p. 2.

[15] St Mary's Willesden PR for baptisms of William (18 January 1746) and Robert (16 December 1750), respectively the third and fourth sons of John and Mary Marsh, and for John Marsh's second marriage; he and Ann, his first wife, had two sons and two daughters. The wills of William and Robert Marsh (proved 27 September 1787 and 25 June 1800 respectively) give detailed information on the brothers' occupations, preoccupations and dependants as well as their financial positions. Both are PCC Wills (available online).

[16] St Botolph's Aldgate PR (marriage of William Marsh and Eleanor Unwin, 3 November 1770); St George's Holborn PR 1773–81 for their children's baptismal records and Eleanor's burial (6 April 1781). St George's Holborn PR for marriage of William Marsh and Jane Stalker (21 February 1784).

[17] Chelsea Poor Rate tax book from 1797 (Christmas qtr., Pt. II, p. 3) to 1798 (Christmas qtr., p. 92).

[18] See wills of William and Robert Marsh, as in n. 15.

[19] Eleanor was baptised 22 March 1781 (St George's Bloomsbury PR). The Navy Lists name Robert Marsh as Purser of the *Queen Charlotte* (which was on station in the Mediterranean) up to and including July 1799. It

has not been possible to establish when he died; the date and cause of his death would have been recorded in the captain's logbook, but on 13 March 1800 the *Queen Charlotte* caught fire, exploded and sank off Livorno, with the loss of 640 men including the captain – and his logbook. H. G. Thursfield, *Five Naval Journals 1789–1817* (London: Navy Records Society, 1951), p. 72.

20 See Thomas Richards, *Wales under the Penal Code 1662–1687* (London: National Eisteddfod Association, 1925), p. 21; W. S. K. Thomas, *Stuart Wales 1603–1714* (Llandysul: Gomer, 1988), p. 125; Geraint H. Jenkins, *The Foundations of Modern Wales 1642–1780* (Oxford: Clarendon Press, 1987), p. 186.

21 Will of Henry Williams of Evenjobb, made 18 July 1800, proved 22 December 1800 (held in Herefordshire County Archives).

22 NLW MS 24052F, f. 82 gives the relevant family tree. David Williams's surviving older brother, Hugh Stephens Williams, died before him (Hugh Stephens Williams 'of Whitney' buried 20 August 1826, New Radnor PR).

23 Old Radnor PR (baptised 16 April 1782).

24 Will of Henry Williams of Evenjobb (see n. 21).

25 ADM 7/817, f. 17; 7/818, f. 102; 7/20, ff. 35–6; 7/820, f. 33–5 for David Williams's employment record. His sister Elizabeth married Henry Hunter Williams on 11 April 1799 (Whitney PR) just over two months before he started work at the Navy Office in London (ADM 7/818, f. 102).

26 When David Williams's eldest sister Ann married for the second time, he and Eleanor and Elizabeth Marsh were the witnesses (12 June 1802, Whitney PR).

27 David Williams and Eleanor Marsh were married on 28 April 1803 (St Mary Abbotts, Kensington PR). Jane Marsh (Eleanor's stepmother) was the householder responsible for paying the Poor Rate tax up to and including the first quarter of 1803; in the tax records for the following quarter her name has been written in as before, then crossed out and 'David Williams' written next to it (Chelsea Poor Rate tax books, 1803 Midsummer qtr, Pt. II, p. 24).

28 From the first quarter of 1817 to the second quarter of 1819, David Williams was the householder at 12 Riley Street (though the number was sometimes recorded as 13; see Chelsea Poor Rate tax books for this period).

29 Jane Williams's sisters Elizabeth and Mary Ann were born on 18 May 1810 and 4 June 1813 respectively in Southsea (St Mary's PR); her brother Edward was born at Queensborough, Sheerness on 26 September

1816 (PR). The family returned to live in London in 1817 (Chelsea Poor Rate tax books, Lady Day qtr. 1817, Pt. 1, p. 4).

30 See ADM files as in n. 25.

31 RLF MS, p. 6

32 The Chelsea Poor Rate tax books for the first two quarters of 1820 show David Williams paying the tax in the usual way. For the third (Michaelmas) quarter his name has been entered as before, then crossed out in different ink and the letter 'E' – the tax clerk's code for 'Empty' – written next to it. This indicates that after he had paid the tax in advance as usual, he and his family left the house before the beginning of the third quarter (i.e. 1 July) and had the tax for that quarter refunded, and that the house was subsequently unoccupied.

33 Jane Williams, *Miscellaneous Poems* (Brecknock: printed by Priscilla Hughes, 1824), p. vii.

34 David Williams's youngest sister Mary married Richard Higgins (17 December 1801; Whitney PR); they lived at Middlewood, Clifford (Herefordshire) and were joined there by her unmarried sister Margaret; see Clifford PR 13 April 1838 and will of Richard Higgins the younger (PCC; PROB 11/2043).

35 See list of subscribers to *Miscellaneous Poems* (Williams, pp. iii–vi) and list of investors in C. R. Clinker, *The Hay Railway* (Dawlish: David and Charles Ltd, 1960), pp. 54–55).

36 Lord and Lady Hereford lived at Tregoyd, near Glasbury (William H. Smith, p. 14); he was chairman of the Hay railway board (Clinker, *The Hay Railway*, p. 38). See the 1841 tithe map for Talgarth in conjunction with the list of owners of its parcels of land for Lord Ashburnham's ownership of Aberenig House (AC 752, Powys County Archives).

37 Glasbury PR shows nine children of James and Mary Anne Morgan baptised 1823–38.

38 Alexis Easley, 'Making a debut', in Linda H. Peterson (ed.), *The Cambridge Companion to Victorian Women's Writing* (Cambridge: Cambridge University Press, 2015), p. 15; Sarah Prescott, *Women, Authorship and Literary Culture 1690–1740* (Basingstoke: Palgrave Macmillan, 2003), pp. 125, 129; David Finkelstein and Alistair McCleery, *The book history reader* (Abingdon: Routledge, 2nd edn, 2006), pp. 326, 18; Isobel Armstrong and Virginia Blain (eds) *Women's Poetry in the Enlightenment: the Making of a Canon 1730–1820* (London: Macmillan, 1999), p. xxx.

39 See, for example, Evan Evans's acknowledged quotations from Gray's 'The Bard' in his 'Paraphrase of the 137th Psalm' (Evan Evans, *Some Specimens of the Poetry of the Ancient Welsh Bards translated into English*

(Llanidloes: John Pryse, 1862), p. 145, ll. 47, 73–4); Elizabeth Edwards (ed.), *Beaumaris Bay and Other Poems*, (Nottingham: Trent Editions, 2016) p. 142, for Richard Llwyd's quotations from Gray, Milton and Shakespeare.

40 See Evan Evans's English translation of his englynion 'Llys Ifor Hael', p. 148 (according to D. Silvan Evans, the Welsh original was published in 1793), and John Dyer's 'Grongar Hill', in *The Poems of John Dyer*, ed. Edward Thomas (London: T. Fisher Unwin, 1903), ll. 72–90.

41 William Owen Pughe, *The Heroic Elegies and Other Pieces of Llywarç Hen* (London: printed for J. Owen and E. Williams, 1792), translations of the elegies for Cynddylan (esp. pp. 77–81), and Urien Rheged (esp. pp. 39–43).

42 Mrs M. L. Dawson, 'Notes on the History of Glasbury', *Archaeologia Cambrensis*, XVIII (sixth series, 1918), 279–319, pp. 301, 304; E. P. Jones, 'Cartrefi Enwogion Sir Frycheiniog', *Brycheiniog* Vol. XII (1968/69), pp. 107–153.

43 Edward Jones, pp. 42ff.:

Nature herself is changed, and lo!
How all things sympathise below! . . .
Hark! how the sullen tempests roar!
See! how the white waves lash the shore!
See! how eclipsed the sun appears!
See! how the stars fall from their spheres! . . .
Why are we left to mourn in vain,
The guardian of our country slain?
No place, no refuge for us left,
Of homes, of liberty bereft;
Where shall we flee? To whom complain
Since our dear Llewelyn's slain.

44 Lee Erickson, 'The Market', Richard Cronin et al. (eds), *A Companion to Victorian Poetry* (Oxford: Blackwell, 2002), p. 345.

45 *OED*, vol. II, p. 706; Jessica Gerard, *Country House Life: Family and Servants, 1815–1914* (Oxford: Blackwell, 1994), pp. 165, 223, 257; see also Leonore Davidoff and Catherine Hall, *Family Fortunes: Men and Women of the English Middle Class 1780–1850* (1987; revised edn, Abingdon: Routledge, 2002), p. xxxvii; Amanda Vickery, *The Gentleman's Daughter: Women's Lives in Georgian England* (New Haven, London: Yale University Press, 1998), pp. 182, 271.

46 Aberllynfi House is described as 'an attractive and dignified building of considerable architectural merit' with a 'spacious entrance hall and

good [eighteenth-century] staircase' (S. R. Jones, 'The Houses of Breconshire' (Part II), *Brycheiniog*, X (1964), 69–183. pp. 106–7).

[47] Wills of Isabella Hughes (PCC; PROB 11/2021), Rev. John Hughes, (PCC; PROB 11/1497).

[48] Jane Marsh's will, proved 21 March 1844; see affidavit of Isabella Hughes, (PROB 11/1995).

[49] There is an interesting comparison with the way Richard Llwyd gained access to the books and manuscripts in his employers' libraries while he was working as a domestic servant and steward; see Richard Llwyd, *The Poetical Works of Richard Llwyd the Bard of Snowdon* (London: Whittaker and Co., 1837), pp. xl–xli, and Edwards in Llwyd, *Beaumaris Bay* (2016), p. xxi.

[50] Jane Williams, *The Literary Remains of the Rev. Thomas Price Carnhuanawc* (Crickhowell: Thomas Williams, vol. 2 (1855), pp. 264–8.

[51] Jane Williams, *Brief Remarks on a Tract entitled 'A Call to the Converted'* [abridged] (Hereford: T. T. Davies, 1839), p. 16.

[52] Williams, *Brief Remarks*, p. 23.

[53] Williams, *Brief Remarks*, p. 23.

[54] See Isabella Hughes's will (n. 46).

2

[1] Saunders, *Louisa Stuart Costello*, p. 10.

[2] See Sarah Prescott, *Women, Authorship and Literary Culture 1690–1740* for a general discussion of the role of patronage in women's writing careers, and Easley, 'Making a debut' p. 15.

[3] Prescott (2003), *Women, Authorship and Literary Culture*, p. 116.

[4] Prescott (2003), *Women, Authorship and Literary Culture*, p. 117.

[5] Johnston, *Anna Jameson*, pp. 2–3; Saunders, p. 8.

[6] See Celyn Gurden-Williams, 2008; Rachel Ley, 2001; Prys Morgan, *Gwenynen Gwent* (Darlith yn yr Eisteddfod Genedlaethol Casnewydd, 1988); Freeman, 'Lady Llanover and the Welsh ostume prints', *National Library of Wales Journal*, 34/2 (2007), 1–18.

[7] Margaret Mostyn, who worked at Llanover as a maid in 1861–2, commented that many of the recipients 'evidently . . . had not worn [their Welsh costume] since the last time they came for their clothing' (NLW MS 23511A, 20, 1861).

[8] Prys Morgan, *Gwenynen Gwent*, p. 5; Llanover Court was built "mewn arddull Duduraidd ramantus" (in a romantically Tudor style).

[9] Prys Morgan, *Gwenynen Gwent*, p. 10. See also Maxwell Fraser, 'Lady Llanover and her Circle', *Transactions of the Honourable Society of*

Cymmrodorion, Part II (1968), 170–96, Siân Rhiannon Williams, 'Llwydlas, Gwenynen Gwent a dadeni Diwylliannol y Bedwaredd Ganrif ar Bymtheg', *Cof Cenedl XV* (gol. Geraint H. Jenkins) (Llandysul: Gwasg Gomer, 2000), *passim*, and Jane Williams's letters when staying at Llanover Court (NLW MS 26/9).

10 NLW MS 26/9 10 October 1851; 2 October 1852.

11 NLW MS 26/9 30 September 1852.

12 NLW MS 26/9 27 March, 1854.

13 NLW MS 26/9 26 February 31 March 1854; 10 October 1851.

14 NLW MS 26/9 (14 March 1854).

15 See Gareth D. Evans, *A History of Wales 1815–1906* (Cardiff: University of Wales Press, 1989); David Jones, *Before Rebecca: Popular Protest in Wales 1783–1835* (London: Allen Lane/University of Wales Press, 1975); Pat Molloy, *And They Blessed Rebecca* (Llandysul: Gomer, 1981); Kenneth Morgan, *Wales 1890–1980: Rebirth of a Nation* (Oxford: Oxford and Wales University Presses, 1982); John Davies, *Hanes Cymru* (London: Allen Lane/Penguin, 1990); Gwyn A. Williams, *The Merthyr Rising* (Cardiff: University of Wales Press, 1978).

16 Quoted in Ivor Wilks, *South Wales and the Rising of 1839* (London: Croom Helm, 1978), p. 26.

17 *Hansard*, vol. XXIV (1846), p. 846.

18 See Gwyneth Tyson Roberts, *The Language of the Blue Books: Wales and Colonial Prejudice* (Cardiff: University of Wales Press, 1998, 2011) for a detailed account.

19 Quoted in Frank Smith *The Life and Work of Sir James Kay-Shuttleworth* (first edn. London: Murray, 1923), pp. 202–3.

20 *Report on Education in Wales* I, 7; II, 66; III, 63.

21 For Augusta Hall's part in the publication of *Artegall*, see Tonn MS 3.109A; emphasis as in the original. The letters have not been catalogued.

22. Ieuan Gwynedd, p. 33; Owen Owen Roberts, *Education in North Wales* (Caernarfon: James Rees, 1847), p. 7.

23 Jane Williams, *Artegall: or Remarks on the Reports of the Commissioners of Enquiry into the State of Education in Wales* (London: Longman & Co., 1848), p. 5.

24 Williams, *Artegall*, p. 5.

25 Williams, *Artegall*, p. 62.

26 Williams, *Artegall*, pp. 7, 57.

27 Williams, *Artegall*, pp. 53, 56, nn. 40, 44.

28 Williams, *Artegall*, pp. 40, 41, 42–3.

29 Williams, *Artegall*, pp. 54, 36

[30] Williams, *Artegall*, pp. 32, 33.
[31] Williams, *Artegall*, p. 34.
[32] Williams, *Artegall*, p. 48.
[33] See, for example, *Morning Chronicle*, 22 March 1848; *Caernarvon & Denbigh Herald*, 5 April 1848; *Hereford Times*, 8 April 1848; *The Principality*, 5 May, 19 May 1848.
[34] Jane Williams ['The Author of "Artegall"'], *The Welshman*, 29 December 1848, p. 2.
[35] See *The Faerie Queene*, Book V.
[36] Hugh Hughes (1848), cartoon no. 9. See Prys Morgan, 'Pictures for the Millions of Wales 1848: The Political Cartoons of Hugh Hughes', *Transactions of the Honourable Society of Cymmrodorion*, I (1995), 65–80.
[37] Jane Williams, *Cambrian Tales* (London: *Ainsworth's Magazine*, March–December 1849, January–March 1850).
[38] Williams, *Cambrian Tales* (March 1849), p. 258.
[39] The two 'Legends of Llyn Safaddan' and 'A Funeral among the Small People'.
[40] Anna Beale, *Traits and Stories of the Welsh Peasantry* (London: Geo. Routledge and Co., 1849), p. viii.
[41] NLW MS 26/9 (20 October 1851)
[42] See n. 8.
[43] Williams, *Cambrian Tales* (March 1849), p. 258; (September 1849), p. 222.
[44] Williams, *Cambrian Tales* (March 1849), pp. 257, 259–67.
[45] Williams, *Cambrian Tales* (March 1849), p. 257.
[46] NLW MS 26/9 10 March 1854; 2 December 1851; 2 October 1852.
[47] Williams, *Cambrian Tales* (September 1849), pp. 221, 228.
[48] Williams, *Cambrian Tales* (December 1849), p. 495.
[49] Williams, *Cambrian Tales* (August 1849), pp. 130, 136, 137.
[50] Williams, *Cambrian Tales* (August 1849), p. 137.
[51] Williams, *Cambrian Tales* (November 1849), p. 415.
[52] Williams, *Cambrian Tales* (December 1849), p. 496.
[53] Williams, *Cambrian Tales* (February 1850), p. 126.
[54] Williams, *Cambrian Tales* (February 1850, p. 131.
[55] Williams, *Cambrian Tales* (July 1849), p. 81
[56] Williams, *Cambrian Tales* (November 1849), p. 417; (October 1849), *passim*; (October 1849), p. 367; (May 1849), *passim*; (1848), pp. 29–30.

3

1 Williams, *Cambrian Tales* (March 1849), p. 267. Given the time required for proofreading, printing, etc., the fact that this tribute appears in the issue of *Ainsworth's Magazine* published four months after his death suggests that it was added to the existing text very late.

2 Williams, *The Literary Remains*, p. ix. Or he may have balked at becoming involved in a project where he would continually have to answer to Augusta Hall. The letters of the Tonn MSS (written at the same period) show that she repeatedly gave him instructions about the establishment and curriculum of Llandovery College, expected to see in advance his letters to the press about *Artegall*, and then 'could not resist rewriting' them. She also held strong views against absentee clergy in Welsh parishes, and in the list of subscribers to the *Literary Remains* of Carnhuanawc the Archdeacon's address is given (entirely unnecessarily) as 'Brighton' (Jane Williams, 1854, p. 394). In *Cambrian Tales*, the 'Venerable Archdeacon of Llandim' (*sic*) argues with Lady Jeffreys and receives a sharp verbal rap over the knuckles for it; and when Lady Edith asks why the Welsh parson – good-hearted, humble and committed to the welfare of his parishioners – does not hold the living of the parish, the Archdeacon 'with a sour smile' answers, 'Because it is mine' (Williams, March 1849, pp. 258, 267).

3 Williams, *The Literary Remains* (1854), pp. 393-400.

4 Williams, *The Literary Remains* (1855), p. xi.

5 Williams, *The Literary Remains*, p. x; (vol.1, 1854), p. xi; (vol.2, 1855), p. xi.

6 Saunders Lewis, 'Y Cofiant Cymraeg', *Meistri'r Canrifoedd* (gol.) Geraint Gruffudd (Caerdydd: Gwasg Prifysgol Cymru, 1983), 341–56.

7 Williams, *The Literary Remains* (1855), p. 46.

8 Williams, *The Literary Remains* (1855), pp. 68–71.

9 Williams, *The Literary Remains* (1855), pp. 71, 89.

10 Williams, *The Literary Remains* (1855), pp. 128, 138.

11 Williams, *The Literary Remains* (1855), pp. 374–80.

12 John Hughes [Ceiriog], *Oriau'r Hwyr* (Wrexham: Hughes and Son, 1872), pp. 78–9. 'Y mae yn nhy/Syr Harri Ddu/Delyn aur a thanau rhawn/Telyn hen y teulu /Hen alawon annwyl/Yn ei syml swyn/ Hen arferion gwledig.//Boneddwr cu/Yw Syr Harri Ddu/Hoff o'i wlad ac hoff o'i iaith' (In the house/of Syr Harri Ddu/was a gold harp with horsehair strings/old harp of the family/beloved old songs/in

its simple enchantment/old country customs. //A beloved gentleman/ is Syr Harri Ddu /who loved his country and its language).

13 Williams, *The Literary Remains* (1855), pp. 412–13.

14 Giraldus Cambrensis, *The Journey through Wales* (trans. Sir Richard Colt Hoare) (1806; New York: AMS Press, 1968), p. 274.

15 Jane Williams, *The Literary Remains* (1855), pp. 3, 9.

16 Williams, *The Literary Remains* (1855), p. 346.

17 Williams, *The Literary Remains* (1855), pp. 24–39.

18 Williams, *The Origin, Rise and Progress of the Paper People* (London: Grant and Griffith, 1856), p. 15.

19 Williams, *The Origin, Rise and Progress of the Paper People*, pp. 2, 4, 6, 3, 4.

20 Williams, *The Origin, Rise and Progress of the Paper People*, pp. 18, 10.

21 Williams, *The Origin, Rise and Progress of the Paper People*, p. 10.

22 Williams, *The Origin, Rise and Progress of the Paper People*, p. 17.

23 Williams, *The Origin, Rise and Progress of the Paper People*, p. 13.

24 Williams, *The Origin, Rise and Progress of the Paper People*, pp. 13, 21.

25 RLF MS, p. 5.

26 Barbara Denny, *Chelsea Past* (London: Historical Publications, 1996), pp. 92–104, 61, 64.

27 NLW MS 26/9, 23 March 1854.

28 Glansevern MSS 3880 (in NLW).

29 1851 Census (Neuadd Felen, Talgarth, Brecs.); death certificate of Williams's mother, 4 June 1851; marriage certificate of Edward Williams and Catherine Fletcher, 27 June 1854.

30 See n. 23; RLF MS, pp. 2, 6, 8.

31 Jane Williams, *The Autobiography of Elizabeth Davis a Balaclava Nurse*, 2 vols (London: Hurst and Blackett, 1857; reissued Dinas Powys: Honno, 2015), pp. 239–40.

32 LD/FNM/0073, p. 10.

33 Williams, *The Autobiography of Elizabeth Davis*, pp. 298, 304.

34 Williams, *The Autobiography of Elizabeth Davis*, p. 147.

35 Williams, *The Autobiography of Elizabeth Davis*, pp. 18–19.

36 Some writers take the autobiography as a work of oral history: Terry Breverton *100 Great Welsh Women* (1995), p. 23. The *DWB* says it was 'compiled' by Jane Williams without specifying where she obtained the material. Others say that Cadwaladr wrote her own autobiography with Williams's editorial help: L. Twiston Davies and Avery I. Edwards *Women of Wales* (1935), p. 266; Rob Davies 'A nursing legend . . .', *Daily Post*, 28 January 2013, p. 19. Still others omit any mention of Williams and imply that Cadwaladr wrote her autobiography without any help:

Harri Parri, *O'r Bala i'r Balaclafa* (1994) and Helen Emanuel Davies, 'Cymraes y Crimea: Hanes Betsi Cadwaladr', *Y Wawr*, Rhif 149 (Gaeaf 2005), p. 13.

37 Martin Hewitt, 'Diary, Autobiography and the Practice of Life History', in Amigoni, pp. 21–39 (2006); Linda H. Peterson *Traditions of Women's Autobiography: the Practice and Politics of Life Writing* (Charlottesville: University Press of Virginia, 1999), p. x; Estelle C. Jelinek, *The Tradition of Women's Autobiography from Antiquity to the Present* (Boston: Twayne Publishers, 1980), p. 4.

38 Amigoni, pp. 5, 21.

39 Sarah Stickney Ellis: quoted in Valerie Sanders, *The Private Lives of Victorian Women: Autobiography In Nineteenth-Century England* (Hemel Hempstead; Harvester Wheatsheaf, 1989), p.7.

40 Stuart Miller, *The Picaresque Novel* (Cleveland, London: Press of Case Western Reserve University, 1967), p. 13; see also Alexander A. Parker, *Literature and the Delinquent: The Picaresque Novel in Spain and Europe 1599–1753* (Edinburgh: University of Edinburgh Press, 1967) and Francisco Rico, trans. Charles Davies *The Spanish Picaresque Novel and the Point of View* (Cambridge: Cambridge University Press, 1984).

41 Williams, *The Autobiography of Elizabeth Davis*, p. 59.

42 Williams, *The Autobiography of Elizabeth Davis*, pp. 88, 98.

43 Williams, *The Autobiography of Elizabeth Davis*, p. 186.

44 Williams, *The Autobiography of Elizabeth Davis*, p. 241; LD/FNM/0073, p. 10.

45 Williams, *The Autobiography of Elizabeth Davis*, p. 17.

46 Williams, *The Autobiography of Elizabeth Davis*, p. 18.

47 Gruffydd Jones, 'The Incredible Adventures of Betsi Cadwaladr: "Welsh Florence Nightingale" or "Munchausen in Petticoats"? An Evaluation of *The Autobiography of Elizabeth Davis* as a historical source' (Open Resource Online, 2019) esp. pp. 14–20.

48 Llanycil PR (burial), 10 February 1800.

49 Williams, *The Autobiography of Elizabeth Davis*, p. 43; Llanycil PR (baptism), 24 May 1789.

50 LD/FNM/0073, p.10.

51 Bostridge, p. 269. Selina Bracebridge, one of Nightingale's closest friends and her personal assistant at Scutari, described Cadwaladr's *Autobiography* as 'that odious, lying book' without making it clear whether this was an accusation of specific lies or more general distaste for a book which presented Nightingale unsympathetically.

52 Williams, *The Autobiography of Elizabeth Davis*, p. 69.

[53] Williams, *The Autobiography of Elizabeth Davis*, p. 108.
[54] Williams, *The Autobiography of Elizabeth Davis*, pp. 148, 205.
[55] See n. 35.
[56] Williams, *The Autobiography of Elizabeth Davis*, pp. 24–41.
[57] Williams, *The Autobiography of Elizabeth Davis*, p. 317,
[58] Williams, *The Autobiography of Elizabeth Davis*, p. 18. The National Archives website has a link to a letter from Elizabeth Davis applying to become one of Nightingale's nurses which the Archive's accompanying material attributes to Betsi Cadwaladr. The attribution is unconvincing, not only because of the writer's personal details (she was forty-four years old, the widow of an engineer, and lived in Southampton) but because the date of the letter (21 November 1854) means that there would not have been time for her to have been interviewed and her application processed before the second party of nurses (of whom Cadwaladr was one) assembled in London on 1 December to leave for Turkey. Elizabeth Davi(e)s was a very popular name during that period, as anyone who has spent time searching for traces of Cadwaladr in the public records of this period can testify.

4

[1] Jane Williams, *The Literary Women of England, including a Biographical Epitome of all the Most Eminent to the year 1700, and Sketches of the Poetesses to the year 1850; with Extracts from their Works, and Critical Remarks* (London: Saunders, Otley and Co., 1861), pp. 133, 131.
[2] Williams, *The Literary Women of England*, p. 1.
[3] Williams, *The Literary Women of England*, pp. 366–7.
[4] *The Examiner*, 21 September 1861.
[5] *The Morning Post* 19 September 1861, p. 2.
[6] Williams, *The Literary Women of England*, pp. 2–3.
[7] H. W. Parke *Sibyls and Sibylline Prophecy in Classical Antiquity* (London: Routledge, 1988), pp. 51–67, 80; John R. Bartlett, *Jews in the Hellenistic World* (Cambridge: Cambridge University Press, 1985), p. 35.
[8] Williams, *The Literary Women of England*, pp. 4, 560.
[9] Mrs Roe, *A Woman's Thoughts on the Educating of Girls* (1866); quoted in Deborah Gorham, *The Victorian Girl and the Feminine Ideal* (first publ. Abingdon, 1982; London: Routledge, 2013), p. 104.
[10] Williams, *The Literary Women of England*, pp. 282, 315, 340–1.
[11] Charles Kingsley, *Miscellaneous Poems* (London: John Long, 1908), p. 118. The poem ('A Farewell') was first published in 1856.
[12] Williams, *The Literary Women of England*, pp. 272–4.

[13] Quoted in Davidoff and Hall, *Family Fortunes*, p. 453.
[14] Williams, *The Literary Women of England*, p. 130.
[15] Felicia Hemans, (ed. Susan J. Wolfson) *Felicia Hemans: Selected Poems, Letters, Reception Materials* (Princeton and Oxford: Princeton University Press, 2000), p. 5 (ll. 24, 37–8).
[16] Williams, *The Literary Women of England*, pp. 115, 152, 155.
[17] Williams, *The Literary Women of England*, p. 128.
[18] This incident is described in NLW MS 26/9, 5 October 1851; Lady Morgan is recorded as singing 'The night before Larry was stretched' on 9 October 1851.
[19] Williams, *The Literary Women of England*, pp. 25, 28.
[20] Williams, *The Literary Women of England*, pp. 199, 255; 310, 519; 195, 267; 21; 20–1.
[21] Williams, *The Literary Women of England*, pp. 105, 143, 249, 292.
[22] Williams, *The Literary Women of England*, pp. 482, 437.
[23] Williams, *The Literary Women of England*, pp. 63, 75, 83, 86, 253.
[24] Williams, *The Literary Women of England*, p. 299.
[25] Williams, *The Literary Women of England*, p. 427.
[26] Marion Löffler, *The Literary and Historical Legacy of Iolo Morganwg 1826–1926* (Cardiff: University of Wales Press, 2007), p. 178.
[27] Brynley F. Roberts, '"The Age of Restitution": Taliesin ab Iolo and the reception of Iolo Morganwg', in Jenkins (2009), pp. 461–79, p. 477–8.
[28] Jane Williams, *Celtic Fables, Fairy Tales and Legends, chiefly From Ancient Welsh Originals* (London: no publisher's name, 1862), pp. 20, 25.
[29] Williams, *Celtic Fables*, p. 17.
[30] Cambrensis, *The Journey through Wales*, p. 352.
[31] Robert Hunt, *Popular Romances of the West of England: or, the Drolls, Traditions and Superstitions of Old Cornwall* (London: John Camden Hotten, 1871), p. 108; original emphasis.
[32] Cambrensis, *The Journey through Wales*, p. 391.
[33] Williams, *Celtic Fables*, p. 36.
[34] *GPC*, IV, p. 3829.
[35] Iolo MSS, p. 607.
[36] Jones, *A History of the County of Brecknock*, p. 4.
[37] Williams, *Celtic Fables*, p.47.
[38] Iolo MSS, p. 603.
[39] Iolo MSS, p. 603.
[40] Iolo MSS, p. 603.
[41] Williams, *Celtic Fables*, p. 10.
[42] Williams, *Celtic Fables*, p. 9.
[43] Williams, *Celtic Fables*, p. 14.
[44] Williams, *Celtic Fables*, p. 14.

[45] *Proverbs* 6:6; *Matthew* 25:1–13.
[46] Williams, *Celtic Fables,* p. 28.
[47] *Matthew* 6:34.
[48] Williams, *Celtic Fables,* p. 28.
[49] Williams, *Celtic Fables,* p. 29.
[50] Williams, *Celtic Fables,* p. 28.
[51] Sir Roger L'Estrange, *Fables of Aesop and other Eminent Mythologists: with Morals and Reflexions* (London: D. Brown and others, 1724), p. 236.
[52] Williams, *Celtic Fables,* p. 29.
[53] Mark Loveridge, *A History of Augustan Fable* (Cambridge: Cambridge University Press, 1998), p. 70.
[54] See Jayne Elizabeth Lewis, *The English Fable: Aesop and Literary Culture 1651–1740* (Cambridge: Cambridge University Press, 1996), p. 35; Loveridge, *A History of Augustan Fable,* pp. xii, 32; and Aphra Behn, *The Uncollected Works of Aphra Behn* (ed. Germaine Greer) (Stump Cross, Essex: Stump Cross Books, 1989), especially Fable XXX, p. 81.

5

[1] Williams's death certificate gives the cause of death as 'Dilation of heart and defective action', diagnosed 30 years earlier (death certificate issued 17 March 1885, South Chelsea). I am grateful to Dr Beryl Thomas of Aberystwyth for discussing the medical implications of this condition with me (NLW MSS 26/9, 3 October 1851).
[2] RLF, p. 5.
[3] See Monika Baár, *Historians and Nationalism: East Central Europe in the Nineteenth Century* (Oxford: Oxford University Press, 2010) for a detailed discussion.
[4] David Lowenthal, *The Heritage Crusade and the Spoils of History* (Cambridge: Cambridge University Press, 1997), pp. 107, 120.
[5] Grace Jones, 'Early modern Welsh nationalism and the British history', in *Writing Wales from the Renaissance to Romanticism*, ed. Stewart Mottram and Sarah Prescott (Farnham: Ashgate, 2012), pp. 21–38.
[6] Arthur Marwick, *The New Nature of History: Knowledge, Evidence, Language* (Basingstoke; Palgrave, 2001), p. 74.
[7] William Warrington, *The History of Wales in nine books* (London: J. Johnson, 1786), p. 535.
[8] E. C. Campbell, *Stories from the History of Wales* (Shrewsbury: printed by J. Eddowes, 1833), p. 158.

[9] B. B. Woodward, *The History of Wales from the Earliest Times to its Final Incorporation with the Kingdom of England* (London: James S. Vertue, 1853), p. 240.

[10] Matthew Arnold, *On the Study of Celtic Literature* (London: Smith, Elder and Co., 1867), esp. pp. 180–1.

[11] Jane Williams, *A History of Wales derived from Authentic Sources* (London: Longmans, Green and Co., 1869), p. 255.

[12] Williams, *A History of Wales*, pp. ix, xiii.

[13] Lawrence, p. 125; Maitzen, p. 17.

[14] Baár, *Historians and Nationalism*, p. 52.

[15] Williams, *A History of Wales*, p. 24.

[16] Williams, *A History of Wales*, p. 1.

[17] Williams, *A History of Wales*, pp. 1-2.

[18] John Pointer, *Britannia Romana: or, Roman Antiquities in Britain* (Oxford: Anth. Peisley, 1724), unpaginated Preface (he does not explain why the British have become more 'civiliz'd' than any of the other peoples who formed part of the Roman Empire); John Horsley, *Britannia Romana: or, the Roman Antiquities of Britain in Three Books* (London; John Osborne, Thomas Longman, 1732), pp. 29, 96, *passim.*

[19] 'Ein hynafiaid', 'ein cyndeidiau', 'ein llwyth'; Rev. Thomas Price, *Hanes Cymru: a Chenedl y Cymry, o'r Cynoesoedd hyd at Farwolaeth Llewelyn ap Gruffydd: ynghyd a Rhai Cofiaint Perthynol i'r Amseroedd o'r Fryd Hynny i Waered* (Crickhowell: Thomas Williams, 1842), pp. 1–2 and *passim.*

[20] 'Bwystfil ofnadwy ac erchyll, â'r danedd haearn a [f]wytaodd a dryllio [ynys Prydain' (Price, *Hanes Cymru*, p. 98); 'Notwithstanding his frequent and cruel wars, the civil administration of Agricola first taught the Cymry . . . that a time of peace involved less suffering than a time of active hostility' (Williams, *A History of Wales*, p. 39).

[21] 'Y ffyrdd . . . yn greithiau ar ein gwlad, olion y fflangelliaid' (Price, *Hanes Cymru*, p. 98); 'The roads were planned, cleared and constructed with a view to promote the most direct and convenient communication between the ports, colonies, cities, towns and military stations throughout the country' (Williams, *A History of Wales*, p. 47).

[22] Williams, *A History of Wales*, pp. 46–7.

[23] Williams, *A History of Wales*, p. 39.

[24] Gerald Morgan, p. 37; see also pp. 36, 38, 54, and Geraint H. Jenkins (1987), ch.5, and (1991), *passim.*

[25] See Jane Williams's articles on 'The Welsh Church' in *Daily News*, 5 December 1849; *The Sun*, 3, 9 November, 6, 20, 22 December 1849; 14 January 1850.

[26] Dot Jones, *Statistical Evidence relating to the Welsh Language 1801–1911* (Cardiff: University of Wales Press, 1998), p. 425.

[27] See Geraint H. Jenkins, *The Foundations of Modern Wales 1642–1780* (Oxford: Clarendon Press, 1987), pp. 17, 141–4, 188–9, 372–3.

[28] Paul O'Leary, 'When Was Anti-Catholicism? The Case of Nineteenth- and Twentieth-Century Wales', *Journal of Ecclesiastical History*, 65 (April 2005), 324–6.

[29] Williams, *A History of Wales*, p. 421.

[30] Williams, *A History of Wales*, pp. 207, 225, 272, 274.

[31] Williams, *A History of Wales*, p. 481.

[32] Williams, *A History of Wales*, p. 481.

[33] Williams, *A History of Wales*, p. 43.

[34] Williams, *A History of Wales*, p. 483.

[35] John Davies, *Hanes Cymru* (London: Allen Lane/Penguin, 1990), p. 232; Gwyn A. Williams, *When Was Wales? A History of the Welsh* (London; Penguin, 1985), p. 121.

[36] Jane Williams, *History of Wales* (1869), pp. 490, 481.

[37] Jane Williams, *Literary Women of England* (1861), p. 67.

[38] Williams, *A History of Wales*, p. 495.

[39] NLW MSS 24051 F, ff. 58–108, esp. f. 82.

[40] Jane Williams, 'Henry Williams of Ysgafell in the Parish of Llanllwchaiarn and County of Montgomery', *Transactions of the Powys-Land Club*, IV (1871), 169–80, p. 179.

[41] See Richards, *Wales under the Penal Code*, p. 21; W. S. K., Thomas, *Stuart Wales*, p. 125; Jenkins, *The Foundations of Modern Wales*, p. 186.

[42] See Vavasor Powell, *The Bird in the Cage, Chirping* (1661) and *Hanes Bywyd a Marwolaeth y Parch. Fafasour Powel y Gweinidog a'r Milwr dewrych hwnw a eiddo Iesu Grist* (Dolgellau: John Jones, *c.*1815), for example.

[43] Williams, 'Henry Williams of Ysgafell', p. 171.

[44] Williams, 'Henry Williams of Ysgafell', pp. 177, 180.

[45] Williams, 'Henry Williams of Ysgafell', p. 180.

[46] See wills of Elizabeth Marsh (proved 8 April 1865), Eleanor Williams (proved 18 December 1871) and Elizabeth Williams (proved 18 May 1883).

[47] Jane Williams's will (made 24 October 1883, proved 28 March 1885) refers by name to each of the children of her brother Henry and to each of his children's children, but refers only to 'the children of my Brother Robert Marsh Williams deceased'; she was apparently unable to remember them individually.

48 Jane Williams's will (as in n. 47).

49 The burials of Jane Williams and Mary Willey in Brompton Cemetery are listed in the cemetery's records as BR 126328 and BR127874 respectively.

50 Williams's grave was dug to the standard depth of 6′ 6″, which allows for a second coffin to be buried on top of the first if that is what turns out to be required; the grave is then reopened to a depth of 5′ (letter from M. R. Tiffin, Supervisor of Brompton Cemetery, 11 October 2000). If it is planned from the outset that two coffins shall be buried in the same grave, it is dug to double depth.

51 See details of Jane Williams's will in n. 47.

52 See Shattock, pp. 32–7 and Linda K. Hughes, pp. 287–95; RLF MS, p. 2; NLW MS 26/9.

53 See Aaron, *Pur fel y Dur*, pp. 132–45, 216.

54 NLW MS 26/9, 28 February 1854.

55 Bryan Martin Davies, *Deuoliaethau* (Llandysul: Gomer, 1976), p. 47.

56 Jane Williams's oldest brother, Henry David, who was a lieutenant in the British army, died from a heart attack aged thirty-six; his widow Caroline petitioned for financial help from the army. He was stationed at Chatham Barracks, and his death notice in the local paper says he died there (*Rochester, Chatham and Strood Gazette and Weekly Advertiser*, 16 February 1841); however, his death certificate (7 February 1841) shows that he died in a house in the red-light district of Gillingham (Garden Street, Brompton) at 4.15 a.m. – very unusually, the time of death is given – in the company of Ann Short, who could not write (she made her mark) and was later to be found working for a brothel-keeper in London (1851 Census, 3 Hurst Street, Covent Garden). At the time of Henry David's death, his wife Caroline was approximately seven months pregnant with their fourth child.

Jane Williams's second brother, Edward, was a solicitor, who died aged 59 from chronic alcoholism, as mentioned in Chapter 3. His assets at the time of his death amounted to little more than the value of his and his wife Catherine's possessions and the furniture of their rented house, Neuadd Felen in Talgarth (he did not leave a will – an interesting move for a solicitor). He was known in Talgarth as 'Major' Williams (Fraser, 1961, p. 112), and was described in this way on his tombstone in Talgarth churchyard (*Monumental Inscriptions, St Gwendoline's Parish Church, Talgarth*), Vol. I, (Powys Family History Society, 1996), p. 18, no. 106). He was an officer in the Herefordshire Militia for twenty-seven years; for the final twelve months of his service he is described in the

Militia records as 'Honorary Major' (i.e. not a full major; WO 98/279). Militia ranks were not to be used outside the militia except with specific permission, which the Herefordshire Militia records make clear he had not been given.

Jane Williams's youngest brother, Robert, is described on census returns as a 'Medical Assistant'; this was not a recognised grade and does not indicate medical qualifications. He died aged 58 in Taibach, where he had lived for most of his adult life; the causes of death include 'Chronic bronchitis', 'Abscess of ear' and 'Exhaustion'. He left six children under eighteen; his wife Elizabeth and their infant daughter Margaret had died during the previous two years. At the time of his death he was heavily in debt, and one of his creditors, a grocer, was permitted by the probate court to take his few assets, so that his children got nothing. I have not been able to trace conclusively what happened to his older children; the two youngest, Caroline and Mary Anne, were sent to an orphanage in Bristol (1881 Census, The New Orphanage, St James and St Paul, Bristol). They were respectively eight and nine years old.

57 RLF MS, p. 5 (original emphasis).

Appendix I

1 RLF MS, p. 2; Chelsea PR tax books, 1806 Lady Day Qtr, Pt. II, p. 31; St Luke's, Chelsea PR records her birth on 1 February 1806; NLW MS 26/9 28 February 1854.

2 Poole, p. 193; Theophilus Jones, p. 50; Matthew Owen, p. 172; Poole, p. 193.

3 *DWB*; Breverton, p. 284; Chris Price, pp. 9–10.

4 *DNB*, Vol. LXI, p. 411.

5 Fraser, pp. 96–7; Breverton, p. 284; Chris Price, pp. 9–10; *DWB*.

6 Jane Williams (1848), p. 32.

7 *DNB*, Vol. LXI, p. 411; *DWB*; Fraser, p. 99; *Oxford Companion*, p. 649; *Gwyddoniadur*, p. 963; Dewi Davies, pp. 21–2; Chris Price, pp. 9–10; Matthias, p. 45.

8 *DNB*, Vol LXI, p. 411; *DWB*; Fraser, p. 99; Chris Price, pp. 9–10; Breverton, p. 284; E. P. Jones, 'Cartrefi Enwogion Sir Frycheiniog', *Brycheiniog* Vol. XIII (1968/69), pp. 126–7, p.118.

9 Williams, *A History of Wales*, p. 24.

Appendix 2

1. Jane Williams, *Twenty Essays on the Practical Improvement of God's Providential Dispensation as Means of Moral Discipline to the Christian* (London: R. B. Seeley and W. Burnside, 1838), p. 20.
2. Williams, *Twenty Essays*, p. 101.
3. Williams, *Twenty Essays*, pp. 45, 105.
4. Williams, *Twenty Essays*, pp. 126, 160

Bibliography

Reference Works Consulted

Dictionary of National Biography (ed.) Sidney Lee (London: Smith, Elder and Co., 1900)

Dictionary of Welsh Biography (available online through the National Library of Wales website)

Geiriadur Prifysgol Cymru (Caerdydd: Gwasg Prifysgol Cymru, 1999–2002)

Gwyddoniadur Cymru (goln.) John Davies, Menna Baines, Nigel Jenkins, Peredur Lynch (Caerdydd: Gwasg Prifysgol Cymru, 2008)

The Oxford Companion to the Literature of Wales (ed.) Meic Stephens (Oxford: Oxford University Press, 1986)

Works by Jane Williams

Artegall: or Remarks on the Reports of the Commissioners of Enquiry into the State of Education in Wales (London: Longman & Co., 1848)

The Autobiography of Elizabeth Davis a Balaclava Nurse, 2 vols (London: Hurst and Blackett, 1857; reissued Dinas Powys: Honno, 2015)

Brief Remarks on a Tract entitled 'A Call to the Converted' [abridged] (Hereford: T. T. Davies, 1839)

Cambrian Tales (London: *Ainsworth's Magazine*, March–December 1849, January–March 1850)

Celtic Fables, Fairy Tales and Legends, chiefly From Ancient Welsh Originals (London: no publisher's name, 1862)

'Henry Williams of Ysgafell in the Parish of Llanllwchaiarn and County of Montgomery', *Transactions of the Powys-Land Club*, IV (1871), 169–80

A History of Wales derived from Authentic Sources (London: Longmans, Green and Co., 1869)

The Literary Women of England, including a Biographical Epitome of all the Most Eminent to the year 1700, and Sketches of the Poetesses to the year 1850; with Extracts from their Works, and Critical Remarks (London: Saunders, Otley and Co., 1861)
The Literary Remains of the Rev. Thomas Price Carnhuanawc (Crickhowell: Thomas Williams, 2 vols (1854–5)
Miscellaneous Poems (Brecknock: printed by Priscilla Hughes, 1824)
The Origin, Rise and Progress of the Paper People (London: Grant and Griffith, 1856)
'Owain Lawgoch' (entered in competition at the 1876 Wrexham Eisteddfod).
'Some Particulars concerning the Parish of Glasbury in the Counties of Brecknock and Radnor, obtained from Authentic Documents, Local Traditions, Books and Personal Observation', *Archaeologia Cambrensis*, I, fourth series (1870), 306–23
Twenty Essays on the Practical Improvement of God's Providential Dispensation as Means of Moral Discipline to the Christian (London: R. B. Seeley and W. Burnside, 1838)

Other Works Consulted

Aaron, Jane *Pur fel y Dur: Y Gymraes yn Llên Menywod y Bedwaredd Ganrif ar Bymtheg* (Caerdydd: Gwasg Prifysgol Cymru, 1998)
Aaron, Jane *Nineteen-Century Women's Writing in Wales: Nation, Gender and Identity* (Cardiff: University of Wales Press, 2007)
Alexander, Christine (ed.) *Tales of Glasstown, Angria and Gondal: Selected Early Writings of the Brontës* (Oxford: Oxford University Press, 2010)
Amigoni, David (ed.) *Life Writing and Victorian Culture* (Aldershot: Ashgate, 2006)
Anon. *Hanes Bywyd a Marwolaeth y Parch. Fafasour Powel y Gweinidog a'r Milwr dewrych hwnw a eiddo Iesu Grist* (Dolgellau: John Jones, *c*.1815)
Armstrong, Isabel and Blain, Virginia (eds) *Women's Poetry in the Enlightenment: The Making of a Canon 1730–1820* (London: Macmillan, 1999)
Arnold, Matthew *On the Study of Celtic Literature* (London: Smith, Elder and Co., 1867)
Baár, Monika *Historians and Nationalism: East Central Europe in the Nineteenth Century* (Oxford: Oxford University Press, 2010)
Bartlett, John R. *Jews in the Hellenistic World* (Cambridge: Cambridge University Press, 1985)

Bassett, T. M. *The Welsh Baptists* (Swansea: Ilston House, 1977)
Beale, Anne *Traits and Stories of the Welsh Peasantry* (London: Geo. Routledge and Co., 1849)
Behn, Aphra *The Uncollected Works of Aphra Behn* (ed. Germaine Greer) (Stump Cross, Essex: Stump Cross Books, 1989)
Bell, Peter *Victorian Women: An Index to Biographies and Memoirs* (Edinburgh: P. Bell, *c.*1989)
Bellamy, Joan, Anne Lawrence, Gill Perry (eds) *Women, Scholarship and Criticism: Gender and Knowledge c.1790–1900* (Manchester: Manchester University Press, 2000)
Bostridge, Mark *Florence Nightingale: The Woman and the Legend* (London: Viking, 2008)
Calamy, Edmund *An Account of the Ministers, Lecturer, Masters and Fellows of Colleges and Schoolmasters, who were Ejected or Silenced after the Restoration*, vol. II, 2nd edn (London: 1713)
Campbell, E. C. *Stories from the History of Wales* (Shrewsbury: printed by J. Eddowes, 1833)
Children, George and Nash, George *The Prehistoric Sites of Breconshire: Ideology, Power and Monument Symbolism* (Little Logaston, Herefordshire: Logaston Press, 2001)
Clinker, C. R. *The Hay Railway* (Dawlish: David and Charles Ltd, 1960)
Cragoe, Matthew *Culture, Politics and National Identity in Wales 1832–1886* (Oxford: Oxford University Press, 2004)
Crosland, T. W. H. *Taffy was a Welshman* (London: Ewart, Seymour & Co., 1912)
Cross, Nigel *The Common Writer: Life in Nineteenth-Century Grub Street* (Cambridge: Cambridge University Press, 1985)
Davidoff, Leonore, and Hall, Catherine *Family Fortunes: Men and Women of the English Middle Class 1780–1850* (1987; revised edn, Abingdon: Routledge, 2002)
Davies, Bryan Martin *Deuoliaethau* (Llandysul: Gomer, 1976)
Davies, Damien Walford *Cartographies of Culture: New Geographies of Welsh Writing in English* (Cardiff: University of Wales Press, 2012)
Davies, D[ewi] *Some Interesting People of Breconshire* (Brecon: the author, 1970)
Davies, John *Hanes Cymru* (London: Allen Lane/Penguin, 1990)
Dawson, Mrs M. L. 'Notes on the History of Glasbury', *Archaeologia Cambrensis*, XVIII (sixth series, 1918), 279–319
Dearnley, Moira *Distant Fields: Eighteenth-Century Fictions of Wales* (Cardiff: University of Wales Press, 2001)

Denny, Barbara *Chelsea Past* (London: Historical Publications, 1996)
Dyer, John *The Poems of John Dyer*, ed. Edward Thomas (London: T. Fisher Unwin, 1903)
Easley, Alexis 'Making a debut', in Linda H. Peterson (ed.) *The Cambridge Companion to Victorian Women's Writing* (Cambridge: Cambridge University Press, 2015), pp. 15–28
Edwards, Elizabeth 'Footnotes to a nation: Richard Llwyd's *Beaumaris Bay* (1800)', in Joanna Fowler and Allen Ingram (eds) *Voice and Context in Eighteenth-Century Verse: Order in Variety* (Basingstoke: Palgrave Macmillan, 2015)
Edwards, Elizabeth 'Introduction', in Llwyd (2016)
Erickson, Lee 'The Market', in Richard Cronin, Alison Chapman, Antony H. Harrison (eds), *A Companion to Victorian Poetry* (Oxford: Blackwell, 2002), pp. 345–360
Evans, Evan *Some Specimens of the Poetry of the Ancient Welsh Bards translated into English* (Llanidloes: John Pryse, 1862)
Evans, Gareth D. *A History of Wales 1815–1906* (Cardiff: University of Wales Press, 1989)
Evans, Neil and Huw Pryce (eds) *Writing a Small Nation's Past: Wales in Comparative Perspective 1850–1950* (Farnham: Ashgate, 2013)
Evans, D. Silvan *Gwaith y Parchedig Evan Evans* (Caernarfon: H. Humphreys, 1876)
Finkelstein, David and Alistair McCleery, *The book history reader* (Abingdon: Routledge, 2nd edn, 2006)
Fisher, Deborah C. *Who's Who in Welsh History* (Swansea: Christopher Davies, 1997)
Fraser, Maxwell 'Jane Williams (Ysgafell) 1805–1885', *Brycheiniog*, VII (1961), 95–114
Fraser, Maxwell 'Lady Llanover and her Circle', *Transactions of the Honourable Society of Cymmrodorion*, , Part II (1968), 170–96
Freeman, Michael 'Lady Llanover and the Welsh ostume prints', *National Library of Wales Journal*, 34/2 (2007), 1–18
Gerard, Jessica *Country House Life: Family and Servants, 1815–1914* (Oxford: Blackwell, 1994)
Gibson, William *The Church of England 1688–1832: Unity and Accord* (London: Routledge, 2001)
Gibson, William and Ingram, Robert G. (eds) *Religious Identities in Britain 1660–1832* (Aldershot: Ashgate, 2005)
Giraldus Cambrensis *The Journey through Wales* (trans. Sir Richard Colt Hoare) (1806; New York: AMS Press, 1968)

Gorham, Deborah *The Victorian Girl and the Feminine Ideal* (first publ. Abingdon, 1982; London: Routledge, 2013)

Gramich, Katie and Catherine Brennan (eds.) *Welsh Women's Poetry 1460–2001* (Dinas Powys: Honno, 2003)

Gurden-Williams, Celyn 'Lady Llanover and the creation of a Welsh utopia' (PhD thesis, Cardiff, 2008)

Hemans, Felicia (ed. Susan J. Wolfson) *Felicia Hemans: Selected Poems, Letters, Reception Materials* (Princeton and Oxford: Princeton University Press, 2000)

Hewitt, Martin (ed.) *Representing Victorian Lives* (Leeds: Leeds Centre for Victorian Studies, 1999)

Hewitt, Martin 'Diary, Autobiography and the Practice of Life History', in Amigoni, pp. 21–39 (2006)

Horsley, John *Britannia Romana: or, the Roman Antiquities of Britain in Three Books* (London; John Osborne, Thomas Longman, 1732)

Hughes, John Ceiriog [Ceiriog] *Oriau'r Hwyr* (Wrexham: Hughes and Son, 1872)

Hughes, Linda K. (ed.) *The Cambridge Companion to Victorian Women's Poetry* (Cambridge: Cambridge University Press, 2019)

Hughes. W. J. *Wales and the Welsh in English Literature from Shakespeare to Scott* (Wrexham, London: Hughes & Son, 1924)

Hunt, Robert *Popular Romances of the West of England: or, the Drolls, Traditions and Superstitions of Old Cornwall* (London: John Camden Hotten, 1871)

Ieuan Gwynedd: see Jones, Evan

Jelinek, Estelle C. *The Tradition of Women's Autobiography from Antiquity to the Present* (Boston: Twayne Publishers, 1980)

Jenkins, Geraint H., *Protestant Dissenters in Wales 1639–1689* (Cardiff: University of Wales Press, 2009)

Jenkins, Geraint H. *The Foundations of Modern Wales 1642–1780* (Oxford: Clarendon Press, 1987)

Jenkins, Geraint H. '"Horrid unintelligible jargon"; the case of Dr Thomas Bowles', *Welsh History Review* 15/4, 494–523

Jenkins, Geraint H. (ed.) *A Rattleskull Genius: The Many Faces of Iolo Morganwg* (Cardiff: University of Wales Press, 2009)

John, Angela V. (ed.) *Our Mothers' Land: Chapters in Welsh Women's History 1830–1939* (Cardiff: University of Wales Press, 2004)

Johnston, Judith *Anna Jameson: Victorian, Feminist, Woman of Letters* (Aldershot: Scolar Press, 1997)

Jones, David *Before Rebecca: Popular Protest in Wales 1783–1835* (London: Allen Lane/University of Wales Press, 1975)

Jones, Dot *Statistical Evidence relating to the Welsh Language 1801–1911* (Cardiff: University of Wales Press, 1998)
Jones E. P., 'Cartrefi Enwogion Sir Frycheiniog', *Brycheiniog*, Vol. XIII (1968/69), 126–53
Jones, Evan [Ieuan Gwynedd] *Facts, Figures and Statements in Illustration of the Dissent and Morality of Wales* (London, 1849)
Jones, Grace 'Early modern Welsh nationalism and the British history', in *Writing Wales from the Renaissance to Romanticism*, ed. Stewart Mottram and Sarah Prescott (Farnham: Ashgate, 2012), pp. 21–38
Jones, Gruffydd 'The Incredible Adventures of Betsi Cadwaladr: "Welsh Florence Nightingale" or "Munchausen in Petticoats"? An Evaluation of *The Autobiography of Elizabeth Davis* as a historical source' (Open Resource Online, 2019)
Jones, S. R. 'The Houses of Breconshire' (Part II), *Brycheiniog*, X (1964), 69–183.
Jones, Theophilus *A History of the County of Brecknock in Two Volumes* (1805–9; Brecknock: Edwin Davies, 1898)
Kingsley, Charles *Miscellaneous Poems* (London: John Long, 1908)
Lawrence, Anne 'Women historians and documentary research', in Bellamy et al, pp. 123–41
L'Estrange, Sir Roger *Fables of Aesop and other Eminent Mythologists: with Morals and Reflexions* (London: D. Brown and others, 1724)
Lewis, Jayne Elizabeth *The English Fable: Aesop and Literary Culture 1651–1740* (Cambridge: Cambridge University Press, 1996)
Lewis, Saunders 'Y Cofiant Cymraeg', *Meistri'r Canrifoedd* (gol.) Geraint Gruffudd (Caerdydd: Gwasg Prifysgol Cymru, 1983), 341–56
Ley, Rachel *Arglwyddes Llanofer Gwenynen Gwent* (Caernarfon: Gwasg Gwynedd, 2001)
Llwyd, Richard *The Poetical Works of Richard Llwyd the Bard of Snowdon* (London: Whittaker and Co., 1837)
Llwyd, Richard *Beaumaris Bay and Other Poems*, ed. Elizabeth Edwards (Nottingham: Trent Editions, 2016)
Löffler, Marion *The Literary and Historical Legacy of Iolo Morganwg 1826–1926* (Cardiff: University of Wales Press, 2007)
Lord, Peter *Words with Pictures: Welsh Images and Images of Wales in the Popular Press, 1640–1860* (Aberystwyth: Planet, 1995)
Loveridge, Mark *A History of Augustan Fable* (Cambridge: Cambridge University Press, 1998)
Lowenthal, David *The Heritage Crusade and the Spoils of History* (Cambridge: Cambridge University Press, 1997)

Maitzen, Rohan Amanda *Gender, Genre and Victorian Historical Writing* (New York and London: Garland Publishing Inc., 1998)

Marwick, Arthur *The New Nature of History: Knowledge, Evidence, Language* (Basingstoke; Palgrave, 2001)

Matthias, Roland 'Poets of Breconshire', *Brycheiniog*, XIX (1980–1), 45.

Miller, Stuart *The Picaresque Novel* (Cleveland, London: Press of Case Western Reserve University, 1967)

Mills, Sara *Discourses of Difference: An Analysis of Women's Travel Writing and Colonialism* (London: Routledge, 1991)

Molloy, Pat *And They Blessed Rebecca* (Llandysul: Gomer, 1981)

Morgan, Gerald *Ieuan Fardd* (Caernarfon: Gwasg Pantycelyn, 1988)

Morgan, Kenneth O. *Wales 1890–1980: Rebirth of a Nation* (Oxford: Oxford and Wales University Presses, 1982)

Morgan, Prys *Gwenynen Gwent* (Darlith yn yr Eisteddfod Genedlaethol Casnewydd, 1988)

Morgan, Prys 'Pictures for the Millions of Wales 1848: The Political Cartoons of Hugh Hughes', *Transactions of the Honourable Society of Cymmrodorion*, I (1995), 65–80

O'Leary, Paul 'When Was Anti-Catholicism? The Case of Nineteenth- and Twentieth-Century Wales', *Journal of Ecclesiastical History*, 65 (April 2005), 324–6

Parke, H. W. *Sibyls and Sibylline Prophecy in Classical Antiquity* (London: Routledge, 1988)

Parker, Alexander A. *Literature and the Delinquent: The Picaresque Novel in Spain and Europe 1599–1753* (Edinburgh: University of Edinburgh Press, 1967)

Peterson, Linda H. *Traditions of Victorian Women's Autobiography: The Poetics and Politics of Life Writing* (Charlottesville: University Press of Virginia, 1999)

Pointer, John *Britannia Romana: or, Roman Antiquities in Britain* (Oxford: Anth. Peisley, 1724)

Poole, Edwin *The Illustrated History and Biography of Brecknockshire from the Earliest Times to the Present Day* (Brecknock; published by the author, 1886)

Powell, Vavasor *The Bird in the Cage, Chirping* (1661)

Prescott, Sarah *Women, Authorship and Literary Culture 1690–1740* (Basingstoke: Palgrave Macmillan, 2003)

Prescott, Sarah *Eighteenth-Century Writing from Wales: Bards and Britons* Cardiff: University of Wales Press, 2008)

Price, Rev. Thomas (Carnhuanawc) *Hanes Cymru: a Chenedl y Cymry, o'r Cynoesoedd hyd at Farwolaeth Llewelyn ap Gruffydd: ynghyd a Rhai*

Cofiaint Perthynol i'r Amseroedd o'r Fryd Hynny i Waered (Crickhowell: Thomas Williams, 1842)

Pryce, Huw *J. E. Lloyd and the Creation of Welsh History: Knowing a Nation's Past* (Cardiff: University of Wales Press, 2011)

[Pughe], William Owen *The Heroic Elegies and Other Pieces of Llywarç Hen* (London: printed for J. Owen and E. Williams, 1792)

Rattersbury, Gordon and Ray Cook *The Hay and Kington Railways* (Mold: Railways and Canals Historical Society, 1996)

Richards, Thomas *Wales under the Penal Code 1662–1687* (London: National Eisteddfod Association, 1925)

Rico, Francisco, trans. Charles Davies *The Spanish Picaresque Novel and the Point of View* (Cambridge: Cambridge University Press, 1984)

Roberts, Alun *Welsh National Heroes* (Talybont: Y Lolfa, 2002)

Roberts, Brynley F. '"The Age of Restitution": Taliesin ab Iolo and the reception of Iolo Morganwg', in Jenkins (2009), pp. 461–79

Roberts, Gwyneth Tyson *The Language of the Blue Books: Wales and Colonial Prejudice* (Cardiff: University of Wales Press, 1998, 2011)

Roberts, Gwyneth Tyson '"The fair sequester'd vale": Two Early Poems of Place by Jane Williams (Ysgafell)', *The International Journal of Welsh Writing in English*, II (Cardiff: University of Wales Press, 2014)

Roberts, Owen Owen *Education in North Wales . . .* (Caernarfon: James Rees, 1847)

Roberts, T. R. *Eminent Welshmen*, vol. I (Cardiff and Merthyr Tydfil: The Educational Publishing Company, 1908)

Rodger, N. A. M. *The Command of the Ocean: A Naval History of Britain 1649–1815* (London: Allen Lane, 2004)

Saunders, Clare Broome *Louisa Stuart Costello: A Nineteenth-Century Writing Life* (Basingstoke: Palgrave Macmillan, 2015)

Schwyzer, Philip *Literature, Nationalism and Memory in Early Modern England and Wales* (Cambridge: Cambridge University Press, 2004)

Selleck, R. J. W. *James Kay-Shuttleworth: Journey of an Outsider* (Ilford: The Woburn Press, 1974)

Shattock, Joanne 'Becoming a professional writer', in Linda H. Peterson (ed.), pp. 29–42

Smith, Frank *The Life and Work of Sir James Kay-Shuttleworth* (first edn London: Murray, 1923; Bath: Cedric Chivers, 1974)

Smith, William H. *The Hereford, Hay and Brecon Branch* (Kidderminster; Kidderminster Railway Museum, 2008)

Sweet, Rosemary *Antiquaries: The Discovery of the Past in Eighteenth-Century Britain* (London, New York: Hambledon Contiuum, 2004)

Thomas, W. S. K. *Stuart Wales 1603–1714* (Llandysul: Gomer, 1988)
Thursfield, H. G. *Five Naval Journals 1789–1817* (London: Navy Records Society, 1951)
Vickery, Amanda *The Gentleman's Daughter: Women's Lives in Georgian England* (New Haven, London: Yale University Press, 1998)
Warrington, William *The History of Wales in nine books* (London: J. Johnson, 1786)
Williams, Gwyn A. *The Merthyr Rising* (Cardiff: University of Wales Press, 1978)
Williams, Gwyn A. *When Was Wales? A History of the Welsh* (London; Penguin, 1985)
Williams, Siân Rhiannon 'Llwydlas, Gwenynen Gwent a dadeni Diwylliannol y Bedwaredd Ganrif ar Bymtheg', *Cof Cenedl XV* (gol. Geraint H. Jenkins) (Llandysul: Gwasg Gomer, 2000)
Williams, Taliesin (ed.) *Iolo Manuscripts: A Selection of Prose and Verse, from the Collection made by the late Edward Williams, Iolo Morganwg, for the Purpose of Forming a Continuation of the Myfyrian Archaeology, and Subsequently Proposed as Materials for a New History of Wales* (Llandovery: Williams Rees for the Welsh Manuscript Society, 1848)
Wilks, Ivor *South Wales and the Rising of 1839* (London: Croom Helm, 1978)
Woodward, B. B. *The History of Wales from the Earliest Times to its Final Incorporation with the Kingdom of England* (London: James S. Vertue, 1853)

INDEX